Top 10
IRA
Mistakes

Avoiding Mistakes Can Save Owners of IRAs, 401(k)s, 403(b)s and other Retirement Plans a Fortune in Taxes, Penalties, Fees and Loads....

David F. Royer

Published by DLCA Enterprises, LLC

Top 10 IRA Mistakes
Copyright © 2011 by David F. Royer

Library of Congress Control Number: 2011930210

This book is intended to help owners of IRAs, 401(k) plans, 403(b) plans and other retirement accounts make informed decisions, avoid costly mistakes, and get the maximum benefits from their retirement savings. The author and publisher have used their best efforts in preparing this book. It is not intended to offer specific financial advice or to replace the advice of your financial advisor, accountant, or attorney. Your financial circumstances and retirement goals are unique. You should consult a financial advisor or other professional advisors before implementing any of the tax-saving ideas presented in this book.

Credits

Editing

Leslie J. Thompson – Senior Editor

Carrie N. Royer – Assistant Editor

Interior Art and Layout

Ken Small/Digital Book Designs

Cover Art and Graphic Design

Sam Brandt

Photos

Franklin D. Roosevelt Library, courtesy of the National Archives and Records Administration.

The Republican Company. All rights reserved. Reprinted with permission.

Printing and Production

Hill Print Solutions, Ltd.

 **David F. Royer** entered the financial services industry in 1969 after completing his military obligation. He began studying the growing IRA distribution market in 2002, and today he is a nationally recognized speaker and trainer on the discipline of qualified retirement plan accumulation and distribution. David's many articles about IRA distribution planning have been published in leading national financial periodicals.

David is focused on helping those who are retired, or planning for retirement, to take advantage of the new tax rules approved in 2002 and beyond. These new rules can turn a modest IRA account into a lifetime of income that can span three generations, ensuring that the accountholder's children and grandchildren will not only have greater financial security, but also remember their benefactor's sacrifices and successes for the rest of their lives.

In 2004, David developed the ultimate IRA distribution training course, The Keys to the IRA Kingdom®, which he teaches nationally. Drawing on years of experience and in-depth research, David educates financial planners in the art of helping their clients get the most out of their IRAs, 401(k)s, and other qualified retirement accounts. Those who attend David's course can help IRA owners avoid unnecessary IRA taxes and IRS penalties. Accountholders who seek out a Trained IRA Advisor can take the appropriate steps to properly structure their IRA for minimum taxes and maximum income.

David teaches a simple lesson:

"The IRS has given IRA owners and their beneficiaries a great gift. They just need a little help to unwrap it!"

NAVIGATING THE RETIREMENT MAZE

The sense of being lost and alone is among the most terrifying feelings imaginable. Picture yourself in a rental car, driving in a major city for the first time. It's the middle of a stormy night, you are completely lost, and the only tool you have to find your way is the address of your destination. You are in a bad part of town, there is no one in sight to offer directions, and your cell phone battery just died.

Just ahead, through the heavy rain, you can barely make out a fork in the road. You must make a decision and you sense that if you take the wrong turn, you might find yourself in a dangerous situation. In that moment you remember the agent behind the rental car counter asking whether you wanted to pay an additional $19.95 to have a navigation system (GPS) included in your rental agreement, and you declined. As the fork in the road draws nearer, you realize that you must make a choice right now and you have no way of knowing which way to turn. This nightmare could have been avoided if you had chosen to get the GPS to help you find your way.

Planning for a secure retirement can also become a nightmare for many people, with today's complexities of IRS regulations and hidden tax traps. Navigating the IRS minefield of rules, deadlines, penalties, and over-taxation is similar to trying to find your way in a strange place without a GPS. Hidden tax traps lurk around every corner, and finding help to get good directions is more challenging today than at any time in the past. When you are retired or planning for retirement, taking the wrong fork in the road can result in costly mistakes that cannot be reversed. This book is your retirement planning GPS and will help you navigate the IRS minefield and avoid making wrong turns that could result in a retirement nightmare.

IRA Myths:

Myth #1 - You Own Your IRA

Nothing could be further from the truth! The reality is that you have a partner, the IRS, aka Uncle Sam. For example, if you have $300,000 in your IRA and you are in a 33% federal income tax bracket, the IRS owns approximately $100,000 of your account, leaving only $200,000 for you. This is the contract IRA owners made with the IRS when they tax-deducted their contributions. It was a simple agreement: you save the tax on the seed but you must now pay the tax on the crop. *Your IRS partner will dictate when you will pay the tax and how much you will pay.* If your tax bracket is increased to 50%, the IRS will own half of your IRA. Anything over 50%, the IRS becomes your senior partner. The same rules apply to 401(k)s, 403(b)s, 457 plans and all other qualified retirement accounts.

Myth #2 - You Can Beat the Tax

Also not true. The only way out of an IRA is through the IRS. The contract with the IRS is air tight. You must begin taking taxable distributions by April 1 of the year after you turn age 70½. *Even at death the IRS will get its pound of flesh.* If you die while owning an IRA or other qualified retirement account, your heirs will inherit the IRA taxes. Either way, the taxes must be paid and the

IRS will tell you when they must be paid and how much the taxes will be. Fortunately, strategies exist that can help put the IRA owner back in control so they can determine when and how much tax will be paid.

Myth #3 - There's Nothing You Can Do About It

This is the biggest myth of all. Even though the IRA owner does not own the entire account and there is no way to beat the taxes on IRA distributions, accountholders can still take strategic steps to increase the income from their IRA and ease the tax burden. This is where the trained IRA advisor can play a big role in guiding you through the IRS maze of regulations, deadlines, and penalties and help you get the most out of your IRAs, 401(k)s, and other retirement accounts.

TABLE OF CONTENTS

Introduction...15

Missing a Required Minimum Distribution........................19

Not Taking Advantage of the "Stretch Option".....................29

Not Properly Designating Beneficiaries...........................37

Not Establishing Separate Accounts...............................49

Putting Too Much of Your IRA at Risk............................53

Overpaying Fees and Loads on IRAs, 401(k) and 403(b) Plans...67

Not Taking Advantage of Tax Saving Strategies....................73

Not Rolling 401(k) or 403(b) Plans to an IRA....................89

Too Many Retirement Accounts....................................95

Not Getting a Second Opinion.....................................107

Bonus Chapter for The Boomer Generation..........................125

Summary...137

INTRODUCTION: A BRIEF HISTORY OF RETIREMENT PLANS IN AMERICA

On August 14, 1935 President Roosevelt signed the Social Security Act into law

This piece of legislation was intended to help Americans supplement their personal retirement savings, not replace it. Federal legislators recognized that American workers were not saving enough and might need government support to ensure they had the basic living necessities during their retirement years. It was never the government's intention to return our income tax dollars so we could retire comfortably at Uncle Sam's expense. In fact, government leaders have struggled with this issue throughout history:

"The national budget must be balanced. Public debt must be reduced. The arrogance of authorities must be moderated and controlled. Payments to foreign governments must be reduced if this nation doesn't want to go bankrupt. People must again learn to work instead of living on public assistance."

Marcus Tullius Cicero, 55 B.C.

To ensure that the money would be available for its intended purpose, President Roosevelt promised that as long as he lived, Americans would pay no income tax on their Social Security benefits. In 1983, Congress broke that promise and today, if you have an income of $25,000 and are single, or a combined income of $32,000 and are married, you will pay income tax on 50% of your Social Security benefit. It gets worse: if you have income of $34,000 and are single, or an income of $44,000 and are married, you will pay income tax on 85% of your Social Security benefit.

Working Americans pay into the Social Security system with after tax dollars, and those who are receiving benefits and continue to have income over the thresholds are also paying income tax on their Social Security benefits. Uncle Sam gets to double-dip, while senior citizens struggle to make ends meet and are left without the safety net the federal legislators originally intended.

The better people do to earn income to support themselves during their retirement years, the more likely they will end up paying income tax on their Social Security benefits. This is important because distributions from a traditional IRA are taxed as ordinary income. Increases in your taxable income can increase the tax on your Social Security benefits.

DAVID F. ROYER

In 1974 Congress passed The Employee Retirement Income Securities Act (ERISA)

This act marked the birth of the modern retirement plans to which many of us have been contributing for 30 years or more. Out of this landmark legislation grew IRAs, 401(k)s and other company sponsored plans, SEPs, 403(b) plans used by educators, and most other qualified retirement plans. ERISA was designed to encourage Americans to prepare for retirement and be less dependent on Uncle Sam.

The government gave Americans four attractive incentives to save:

1. Participants were allowed to deduct their contributions from their taxable income.

2. Their gains were tax deferred.

3. These retirement accounts were exempt from creditors.

4. Payroll deduction for company employees made it much easier to save for retirement.

With all of these enticements, saving for retirement was practically irresistible, and Americans began to put away millions in IRAs and other retirement accounts. But, there was a catch!

These accounts ultimately became a TAX PRISON!

For many, IRAs, 401(k)s and other qualified retirement accounts are the bulk of their retirement savings. These savers made systematic, tax deductible contributions during most of their working lives, and after turning age 70½ they must take systematic, fully taxable withdrawals. It's not uncommon for the current balance in a retirement account to be two or three times the amount deposited over the accountholder's working years. The miracle of compound interest can grow tax-deductible contributions into sizable— and taxable—IRS Nest Eggs. With all of the great tax incentives to save for retirement, Uncle Sam accomplished his goal.

"You saved the TAX on the SEED, but now you must pay the TAX on the CROP."

The good news is that you can take steps to regain control of your IRAs and other retirement plans. This book will help you avoid the IRS tax traps and find the gold nuggets in the tax code that you can use to reduce your tax burden and get the most out of your retirement savings.

— MISTAKE #1 —
MISSING A REQUIRED MINIMUM DISTRIBUTION

This is the #1 and most costly mistake made by IRA owners and their beneficiaries. The first taxable Required Minimum Distribution (RMD) must be taken by April 1 of the year after the IRA owner turns age 70½. This is called the Required Beginning Date (RBD). Future required distributions are based on the account value as of December 31 of the prior year and must be taken by December 31 of the current year. This is how the IRS dictates when the IRA taxes must be paid.

Extreme penalties are charged if the IRA owner fails to take the full RMD by the deadline. **In addition to paying income tax, the owner will also owe an <u>Excise Tax equal to 50% of the missed distribution!</u>** This could create a tax burden of more than 80% on missed Required Minimum Distributions.

Example:

Richard is 79 years old, and his IRA account balance was $500,000 at the end of the prior year. Richard is in a 25% federal income tax bracket. His Required Minimum Distribution (RMD) at age 79 is 5.13% of the $500,000 account balance, as of December 31 of the prior year. That means he must take a taxable distribution of $25,650 (*5.13%* × *$500,000* = *$25,650*) before December 31 of the current year. Richard knew the rules and had every intention of taking his required distribution well before the December 31 deadline. He usually waited until November or early December to take the distribution, so he could earn as much interest as possible before giving the IRS its share. This particular year Richard had some health problems and spent much of his time going back and forth to the doctor's office. In early December, Richard was admitted to the hospital for a needed surgery. All focus was on Richard's health and the last thing on the family's mind was his retirement account. After surgery Richard needed several weeks to recover. Unfortunately, while he was recovering, the December 31 deadline to take the current year's distribution had passed, and Richard failed to withdraw the required amount. This created a big payday for the IRS. Richard now must pay an additional 50% Excise Tax for missing the December 31 deadline, and he will still owe the income tax when the missed distribution is finally taken.

Let's do the math:

$25,650.00 Missed Distribution
-$6,412.50 Income Tax (25%)
-$12,825.00 Excise Tax(50%)
=$6,412.50 Net Distribution for Richard

DAVID F. ROYER

The $25,650 missed distribution minus $6,412.50 Income Tax (25%), minus $12,825 Excise Tax (*half of the missed distribution*) means that **$19,237.50 belongs to the IRS**. Richard is left with only $6,412.50 of the $25,650 required distribution. The IRS took 75% of the missed distribution, due to taxes and penalties, and the IRA owner was left with a mere 25%. If Richard had been in a 33% federal income tax bracket, the IRS would have taken a whopping 83% of the missed distribution. Anytime a Required Minimum Distribution is missed:

"The IRS becomes the IRA owner's Senior Partner!"

Case in Point:

In 2009 I received a call from a financial consultant Alex, who attended my IRA distribution-training course a few months earlier. He wanted to discuss a client he was working with that attended one of his recent financial planning workshops. His client, Mike, was age 77 and had a little more than $600,000 in his IRA. Most of the IRA money had accumulated in his 401(k) while he was working as a supervisor at a sizeable manufacturing plant. When he retired he decided to convert his 401(k) to an IRA, and he set up the IRA in a CD at a local bank. Mike chose the CD so that, unlike his 401(k), there would be no risk. Mike was going to play it safe and make sure his IRA would be there when he needed it.

After Mike retired at age 65, he started a small real estate firm. The real estate market was booming at that time and Mike was making more money selling real estate than when he was employed at the plant. Alex noticed something unusual on his tax returns. There were no withdrawals coming out of his $600,000 IRA and no IRA distribution taxes were paid. Mike had no need to take income from his IRA, so he didn't take the required distributions. Alex pointed this out to Mike and explained that he should have taken his Required Minimum Distribution beginning when he turned 70½ more than six years ago.

Mike replied that the clerk at the bank who sold him the CD years ago said he could keep his money in the bank as long as he wanted to, but didn't explain that he would need to take at least his required distribution each year after turning age 70½. The bank probably sent Mike the annual statement to remind him of his Required Minimum Distribution, as required of IRA custodians, but Mike received so much junk mail from the bank, he threw most of it away unopened.

Mike missed six Required Minimum Distributions that added up to a little more than $150,000. He now owed income tax on the missed distributions (*roughly $50,000*). The income tax will be due when the missed distributions are finally taken. Mike also owes the IRS nearly $75,000 in Excise Tax (*50% of the missed distributions*) in addition to the income tax. The total expense came to more than $125,000, including additional penalties and interest. When all was said and done, Mike got to keep less than $25,000 of the $150,000 of missed distributions.

Mike owed the IRS approximately 83% of the missed distributions in taxes and penalties. This hefty bill from Uncle Sam could have been avoided had Mike received proper advice and set up a formal IRA distribution plan. Not planning cost Mike more than $75,000 of IRS penalties that could have been avoided. Unfortunately, in this case, there was nothing Alex could do to help Mike beat the taxes and penalties. The deadlines for taking Required Minimum Distributions are not flexible and Mike now owed the IRS its pound of flesh.

If you miss the deadline to take your RMD, the best course of action is to take the distribution as soon as you discover your mistake. You can also request a waiver of the 50% Excise Tax by filing a waiver request along with IRS form 5329 explaining the reason for the missed distribution. Some examples of reasons for missing the distribution include:

- The custodian did not process your request before the December 31 deadline.

- The custodian miscalculated the distribution amount.

- The request for the distribution was lost in the mail. (*Good luck with that one*).

- The account owner is elderly or was ill during the year that the RMD was due.

- The IRA owner's spouse usually handled this and he/she was ill or passed away.

The more Required Minimum Distributions you miss, the less likely the IRS will grant you a waiver of the 50% Excise Tax. Don't wait for an audit. After the audit process begins, there is little chance that the IRS will consider a waiver of the penalties.

Beneficiaries also make the mistake of failing to take a Required Minimum Distribution from an inherited IRA

If the beneficiary is your spouse, he or she must decide whether to become the owner of the inherited IRA or remain a beneficiary. Making this choice will determine when distributions are required. If the inheriting spouse chooses to become the owner, distributions can be delayed until he or she reaches age 70½. Additionally, as the new owner, the inheriting spouse can make any needed beneficiary changes.

If an inheriting spouse chooses to remain a beneficiary, he or she must begin taking distributions based on his or her life expectancy, by December 31 of the year following the year of the IRA owner's death, or when the original IRA owner would have turned age 70½, whichever is later. There are times when remaining a beneficiary offers the spouse an advantage. If the spouse is under age 59½ and needs to take distributions prior to age 59½, they will not have to pay the 10% pre-59½ distribution penalty if they remain a beneficiary. Making the decision to become the new owner or remain a beneficiary is an important planning tool for spouses who inherit an IRA.

If the beneficiary is not your spouse, for example if a child, grandchild, or anyone other than the IRA owner's spouse is the beneficiary, they do not have the option of becoming the owner of the inherited IRA. They must remain a beneficiary for the IRA to continue to have tax-deferred status. This is where a non-spousal IRA beneficiary can make an enormous IRA mistake and find themselves in the jaws of one of the most costly IRS tax traps.

Let's consider Jim, who was the beneficiary of his father's $200,000 IRA. Jim had great respect for the sacrifices his father made to save for his retirement years, so when his father died and Jim inherited his father's IRA, he made a commitment not to squander the inheritance that his father worked so hard for. Jim decided to deposit the inherited IRA into his own IRA, and like his father, he would save it for his retirement years. Jim's intentions, admirable as they were, resulted in a tax feast for the IRS.

The moment Jim deposited his father's IRA into his own IRA the entire inherited IRA became immediately taxable. This not only generated a big tax bill for Jim, it also pushed him into a higher tax bracket. Only an inheriting spouse has the option to roll an inherited IRA into their own IRA or become the owner of an inherited IRA. Jim was not informed about the complex IRS rules regarding inheriting an IRA and made the worst possible decision.

For doing something that seemed reasonable, Jim was severely punished. He paid the income tax and a big chunk of his inherited IRA was now the property of the IRS.

Jim should have been better informed about two significant IRS rules:

1. Non-spousal IRA beneficiaries may not become the new owner of an inherited IRA or roll the inherited IRA into their own IRA. If either of these mistakes is made, the inherited IRA will become taxable. Also, unlike spouses who inherit an IRA, non-spousal beneficiaries may not delay taking distributions until they reach age 70½. They must take their first Required Minimum Distribution by December 31 of the year after the IRA owner's death. If this deadline is missed, the non-spousal beneficiaries may be forced to pay all of the IRA taxes in only five years.

2. If the IRA owner was over age 70½ at death and did not take the required distribution during the year of death, the non-spousal beneficiaries, must take a taxable distribution equal to the required distribution the owner would have taken if still

living. If the IRA owner did take the distribution for the year of death, the beneficiaries first Required Minimum Distribution will be based on their life expectancy and must be taken by December 31 of the year after the IRA owner's death. If this deadline is missed, the non-spousal beneficiaries will also be subject to the 50% Excise Tax.

Most non-spousal beneficiaries are not aware of their right to take only the required distributions and keep the majority of the inherited IRA in a tax-deferred status. Taking only the required distribution lets the beneficiaries continue to earn interest on money that would otherwise be paid to the IRS prematurely and enjoy a lifetime of income from their inherited IRA. In Jim's case, in addition to paying an unexpected tax bill, he lost the advantages of the *"Stretch Option"*. The *"Stretch Option"* will be discussed in detail in the next chapter.

With all of the important dates, deadlines, and rules to remember, it is no wonder that failing to take a Required Minimum Distribution is the #1 mistake made by IRA owners and their beneficiaries.

If you miss a Required Minimum Distribution, you have three options:

1. Do nothing and pray you do not get audited by the IRS. If you choose this option and you are audited, the likelihood of the IRS waiving the 50% penalty is slim.

2. Pay the 50% penalty and move on with your life. Giving 50% of the missed distribution to the IRS does not appeal to most IRA owners or their beneficiaries.

3. Take the missed distribution now and request a waiver of the penalty by filing your request, including the reason for missing the distribution, along with IRS form 5329.

Then just wait and keep your fingers crossed.

All of these less-than-attractive options can be avoided with proper planning, including a formal distribution plan for your IRAs and other qualified retirement accounts. Lack of consumer awareness can result in big IRS penalties, additional interest, and over-taxation. Planning now can ensure that you, and your beneficiaries, will not become the junior partner when it's time to take some of your hard-earned money out of your IRAs and other qualified retirement accounts.

— MISTAKE #2 —

NOT TAKING ADVANTAGE OF THE "STRETCH OPTION"

If there is money left in your IRA, who do you want to leave it to and how much do you want to leave to the IRS?

In 2001, the IRS proposed sweeping changes that would create a magnificent financial planning opportunity for owners of IRAs and other qualified retirement plans. These changes went into effect in 2002 and dramatically simplified the complex IRA distribution rules. The new rules were designed, in part, to help prevent owners of retirement plans from outliving their retirement savings, but they did much more. These new rules also created an income planning opportunity that would allow the taxes on IRA distributions to be spread over three generations.

Prior to the new rules, the methods of calculating the Required Minimum Distributions that must begin after age 70½ were complicated. Choosing the wrong method could result in rapid distribution, causing rapid taxation. Even worse, children and grandchildren who might inherit these accounts were forced to pay all of the IRA taxes in one to five years. For many IRA owners and their families, retirement planning became a TAX nightmare.

Beginning in 2002, three major changes created the *"Stretch Option"*

1. The complicated tables for calculating Required Minimum Distributions were reduced to one simple table and a separate table for IRA owners whose spouses are more than 10 years younger.

2. The new distribution rules allowed the IRA owner to take a much smaller distribution, so the IRA could grow faster and last longer. Taking less out of your IRA means less tax today and more money left in these accounts to be passed on to your heirs.

3. Children, grandchildren, and other non-spousal beneficiaries, who are likely to inherit the balance of these accounts, were given the right to spread the distributions and income taxes over their individual life expectancies. They are no longer forced to pay the IRA taxes up front. Prior to this change, IRAs and other retirement accounts became a Tax Time Bomb for inheriting non-spousal beneficiaries, including children and grandchildren. When non-spousal beneficiaries inherit IRAs, they also inherit the IRA taxes. More often than not, the additional income from the inherited IRA forces them into a higher tax bracket. Beginning in 2002, this problem was eliminated and the beneficiaries now have new rights.

They are now able to spread the IRA distributions and taxes over their individual life expectancies. In addition to having the right to turn the inherited IRA into a lifetime of income, they are also able to continue to earn interest on the money that no longer needs to be paid to the IRS prematurely.

This created the *"Stretch Option"* and now a modest IRA can generate a lifetime of income that can span over three generations. This is one of the biggest gold nuggets in the tax code; however, you need to be aware of a few rules to take full advantage of the *"Stretch Option"*.

Owners of IRAs, 401(k)s, 403(b)s, and other qualified retirement accounts have the option to defer taking taxable distributions from their qualified retirement accounts until April 1 of the year after they turn age 70½. This is called the Required Beginning Date (RBD). Spouses who inherit IRAs have the option to become the new IRA owner and delay taking taxable distributions until they reach age 70½, even if this is later than the original owner's Required Beginning Date. The longer the taxable distributions can be delayed, the longer the owner or inheriting spouse can continue to earn tax-deferred interest.

This is not the case when children and grandchildren inherit these same accounts. In 2002 the IRS reduced the amount of the required distributions for IRA owners, so there is a greater likelihood that substantial money will be left in these accounts to be passed on to the children and grandchildren after the IRA owners are gone. This is where a common and costly mistake can be made. Unlike the owners and inheriting spouses, the children/grandchildren cannot delay taking distributions until they turn age 70½. They are required to take at least their Required Minimum Distribution by December 31 of the year after the year of the owner's death.

This minimum distribution must be taken regardless of the ages of the children/grandchildren when they inherit these accounts.

These non-spousal beneficiaries now have the right to spread or *"Stretch"* the distributions over their individual life expectancies and enjoy a lifetime of income from the inherited IRA. Too often, these beneficiaries are not getting adequate advice and make the mistake of missing the required distribution. If the distribution deadline is missed, the beneficiaries may be forced into a lump-sum distribution and wind up paying all of the taxes on the inherited IRA in one to five years.

The following example illustrates the difference between *"Stretch"* distributions and a Lump-Sum distribution

Mr. Jones, a 75-year-old widower, died and left his $100,000 IRA to his 40-year-old son, John. John had a good job and didn't need to use any of the inherited IRA at the moment, so he left the money in the same brokerage account it had always been in. John had no relationship with the broker who handled his father's account and the broker never got around to advising John about his options and deadlines he should be aware of. John's father passed away in December. Thirteen months later, December of the following year had come and gone and John missed the deadline to take his first Required Minimum Distribution. You can guess the rest of the story: The brokerage firm sent John a 1099 for the entire amount of the inherited IRA ($100,000). After paying income tax at John's 33% federal income tax bracket, he had only $67,000 left to spend. *(This is assuming that the account didn't lose any money for that 13-month period.)* Had this scenario happened in 2008, the results would have been nothing less than disastrous.

Here is what would have happened if John had received the advice he needed:

John was 40 when he inherited his father's IRA. Had he chosen the *"Stretch Option"* he would have been able to spread the distributions and the income taxes over 43.6 years, his remaining life expectancy according to *IRS Publication 590*. This would have made it possible for John to continue to earn interest on most of the money he paid to the IRS after a lump-sum distribution. If John earned 5% during the "Stretch" period and withdrew only the annual Required Minimum Distributions, he would have received approximately $355,000 in *"Stretch"* distributions over his lifetime. Even after paying income tax at 33%, he would have more than $234,000 left to spend. $234,000 minus the lump-sum after-tax payment of $67,000 means John would have more than $167,000 additional spendable income with the *"Stretch Option".*

Don't forget the grandchildren!

The younger the IRA beneficiary is, the longer they can defer the IRA taxes. A 40-year-old beneficiary, like John, can spread the distributions and taxes over 43.6 years. A 10-year-old beneficiary can spread the distributions and distribution taxes over 72.8 years. If you haven't considered leaving some of your IRA to your grandchildren, you may be missing the opportunity to defer the taxes even longer.

The following chart illustrates the power of the *"Stretch Option"* in action. In this example, the IRA owner left his $200,000 IRA to his daughter, age 58, and two grandchildren, ages 29 and 25. The daughter inherited 50% ($100,000) and the grandchildren inherited 25% ($50,000) each.

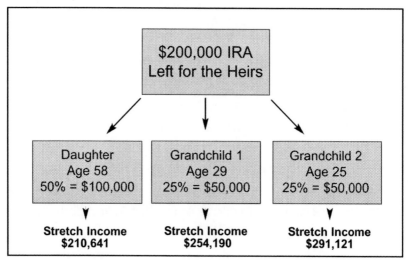

As you can see, the daughter's $100,000 inherited IRA generated more than $210,000 of income over her life expectancy. Both of the grandchildren, who inherited $50,000 each, received incomes in excess of $250,000 *(over five times the amount of IRA money they inherited)*. The combined *Stretch* distributions for the daughter and grandchildren amounted to $755,925 of income from a $200,000 inherited IRA.

The *"Stretch Option"* is a great planning tool for IRA owners who wish to leave their children and grandchildren the legacy of a lifetime of income, rather than an IOU to the IRS.

To accomplish the *"Stretch Option"* the IRA owner must properly designate beneficiaries, and separate accounts must be set up for each beneficiary. Separate accounts can be set up by the owner or by the beneficiaries after the owner's death. These separate accounts, or separate contracts, must be established by December 31 of the year after the IRA owner's death. This will be covered in more detail in the next two chapters.

Let's review the *"Stretch Option"* advantages :

1. **In 2002 the IRS reduced the Required Minimum Distribution for IRA owners.**

This reduction was substantial and cut owners' required distributions almost in half. Taking smaller distributions will lower your tax bill, and may reduce the tax on your Social Security benefits.

2. **If you take less money out of your IRA, more tax-deferred money remains in the account and continues to earn interest.**

The money that would have been paid in taxes stays in the account and continues to grow, meaning there will be more money left in your IRA to be passed on to your spouse or non-spousal beneficiaries *(children and grandchildren).*

3. **Children and grandchildren who inherit what is left in your IRA will also have new and powerful tax advantages.**

They will no longer be forced to pay the IRA taxes in one to five years. Under the new rules they have most of the same distribution rights as the original IRA owner and now can spread the distributions and the taxes over their individual life expectancies. Imagine, if a newborn grandchild inherits part of your IRA, they can spread the distributions and the taxes over the next 82.4 years *(IRS Publication 590 Table-I).* The beneficiary will continue to earn interest on what would have been paid to the IRS.

Proper planning can prevent beneficiaries from making costly IRA mistakes. Missing required distributions from an inherited IRA can result in a lump-sum distribution, accelerated taxation and the loss of the *"Stretch Option".*

— MISTAKE #3 —

NOT PROPERLY
DESIGNATING BENEFICIARIES

The beneficiary form is the single most important document in the estate plan. A common mistake made by retirement plan owners is in the area of beneficiary designations. You would think that choosing who will inherit the money left in your IRA or 401(k) would be simple. The reality is that many children and grandchildren who inherit a qualified plan will be forced into rapid distribution causing rapid taxation due to beneficiary mistakes. Only the IRA owner or inheriting spouse can designate beneficiaries for the purpose of stretching out the distributions and spreading the taxes over the beneficiary's life expectancy. Here are a few common beneficiary mistakes.

Too Much, Too Fast

Younger or less experienced beneficiaries sometimes inherit too much, too fast. *In such cases, the inherited money can do more harm than good!* If the beneficiary has limited experience handling money or has a spendthrift problem, they can squander the funds that were intended to support them throughout their lifetime. Let's face it, the world holds many temptations, and often beneficiaries will quickly burn through their share of the inheritance. It is estimated that the average inheritance in the U.S. is spent within 90 days to 17 months. It's no comfort to the diligent saver to imagine a big chunk of their savings winding up on the tables in Las Vegas or the showroom floor of a new car dealership.

A simple planning tool can prevent this from occurring. IRA owners can choose to restrict a beneficiary, rather than allowing them the option of receiving a fully taxable, lump-sum distribution. In other words, the IRA owner can specify how the money will be paid to a particular beneficiary. Many custodians of retirement funds offer beneficiary documents that allow the owner to choose a payout period. These payout periods can range from five years all the way to life expectancy. In some cases it may be necessary to use a trust, if your custodian does not offer the option of restricting a beneficiary or you desire more control over when and how your beneficiaries can access the funds.

No Contingency Plan

It is common for IRA/401(k) owners to name their spouse as the sole beneficiary of their qualified accounts. As a matter of fact, some states and some custodians require the spouse's consent to name anyone other than the spouse. Naming a contingent beneficiary is also a vital part of effective estate planning. If both the IRA owner and the inheriting spouse are gone, who will receive the balance left in the account? *Business Week Investor* addressed this issue in April 2001:

"It's a little known fact that individual retirement accounts, 401(k)s, and other tax-deferred plans aren't governed by wills or state inheritance laws. Instead, the disposition of your retirement funds depends on two things: the fine print of your Bank or Fund Company's custodial agreement and the tiny lines where you listed beneficiaries."

If the IRA owner fails to designate contingent beneficiaries, the account balance may wind up in probate. Probate can be lengthy and expensive, and during probate the funds are in lock-down. The other problem caused by not designating contingent beneficiaries is the loss of the *"Stretch Option"*. It is necessary for the IRA owner, or inheriting spouse, to name contingent beneficiaries so they can be treated as designated beneficiaries for the purpose of stretching the inherited IRA. This gives the contingent beneficiaries the option to receive the inherited IRA over their life expectancies and enjoy tax deferral as long as possible. The longer the beneficiaries can keep their inheritance tax-deferred, the longer they can continue to earn interest on what otherwise would have been paid to the IRS before it needed to be paid.

Blending Individual
Beneficiaries with Charities

There are four options to consider if you choose to leave all, or some, of your IRA to a qualified charity. Choosing the wrong option can cause big problems for your other non-charity beneficiaries.

1. Name the Charity as 100% IRA Beneficiary.

If you or your family will not need income from your IRA, you may choose to leave the entire amount to the charity of your choice. The charity's advantage is that it will not have to pay taxes on the IRA when it receives the benefit. This way, 100% of your IRA will be available to the charity free from income tax. This is a highly tax-advantaged way for senior IRA owners to fulfill their charitable commitments. Some states and some IRA custodians may require the spouse's consent if the IRA is left to a charity rather than the spouse.

2. Split the Beneficiaries between a Charity and Individual Beneficiaries.

If you want to leave some of your IRA to a charity and the rest to your spouse or children/grandchildren, you could use a single IRA and divide the proceeds with the beneficiary form. This approach could backfire for the children and grandchildren. If the charity does not take full distribution of its share by September 30 of the year after the IRA owner's death, the children and grandchildren could lose the advantage of the *"Stretch Option"*. September 30 is the deadline to determine *"Designated Beneficiaries"* for the purpose of stretching distributions over the beneficiaries' life expectancies. If the charity fails to take a full distribution by the deadline, the *"Stretch Option"* could be lost for your other beneficiaries.

3. Split the IRA into Two IRAs.

This makes a lot more sense than using one IRA for the benefit of a charity and your children, as described above. You can divide your IRA into one IRA for the charity and a second IRA for your other beneficiaries. Using this approach, your children and grandchildren will be able to take advantage of the *"Stretch Option"* without regard to the September 30 deadline for the charity. One less deadline is one less opportunity to make a critical IRA mistake.

4. Set up a Charitable Remainder Trust.

This can be a useful tool if you want to leave income for your spouse as long as he or she is living, and you want whatever is left to go to the charity of your choice. Your spouse will have a lifetime of income from your IRA and at the second death, you will have fulfilled your charitable wishes.

Using a Will to Name Your Beneficiaries

If you use a will to name the beneficiaries of your IRA, the beneficiaries will not be considered *"Designated Beneficiaries"* for the purpose of stretching the distribution over their life expectancies. Instead, if a will is used to name beneficiaries or the IRA owner names their estate, one of the following will occur:

1. If the IRA owner dies prior to age 70½, the entire account must be distributed and all of the taxes paid by December 31 of the fifth anniversary of the IRA owner's death. In simple terms, all the taxes on the inherited IRA will be due in five years.

2. If the IRA owner dies after age 70½, the required distributions can continue to the beneficiaries, but in this case the distributions and tax deferral period will be based on the remaining life expectancy of the IRA owner rather than the longer life expectancy of the younger beneficiary. Either way the beneficiaries lose the advantage of spreading the distributions over their typically longer life expectancy and lose much of the value of the *"Stretch Option"*, as well.

Using a Trust to Designate Multiple Beneficiaries

It is not uncommon for IRA owners to own a trust. It's also not uncommon for them to use the trust to determine who will inherit the balance of their IRAs. This is a frequent, and costly, beneficiary mistake. Most IRA owners will have multiple beneficiaries and they will have different ages. Because of the age difference, they also have different life expectancies and different *"Stretch"* payout periods.

Here is an example of what can happen when you use a trust to designate multiple beneficiaries:

A 45-year-old beneficiary has a *"Stretch"* payout period of 38.8 years, while a 12-year-old beneficiary has a *"Stretch"* payout period of 70.8 years (according to *IRS Publication 590)*. For both of these beneficiaries to be able to use their individual life expectancies for stretching the distributions from an inherited IRA, separate accounts must be established.

Unfortunately, the beneficiaries of a trust cannot use the separate account rule. That means both beneficiaries will be treated as if they are the age of the oldest beneficiary. In this case, the 12-year-old beneficiary will be treated as if they were age 45. This will greatly diminish the payout period and total IRA income for the 12-year-old beneficiary. This will be discussed further in the next chapter.

Not Keeping Your Beneficiary Documents Up-to-Date

Failing to update beneficiary documents is the most common IRA beneficiary mistake.

Circumstances change and when they do, your beneficiary forms may need to be revised. Not keeping your beneficiary forms up-to-date can result in disaster. Here are a few of the triggering events that should alert you that you need to get a beneficiary checkup.

You divorced or remarried

It's not uncommon for an ex-spouse to get an unexpected and pleasant surprise when the IRA owner dies. Why? Because the IRA owner forgot to change the beneficiaries. In this case a new spouse or the IRA owner's children could be disinherited.

A designated beneficiary died or a new potential beneficiary is born

Either way, it's time for a beneficiary check up.

A beneficiary becomes disabled or incompetent and will not be able to manage their inheritance

You may need to consider a trust for the benefit of that beneficiary.

One of your beneficiaries is financially well-off or a beneficiary becomes financially indigent

You may want to adjust the percentages to accommodate real life situations, so you can best provide for loved ones who need financial assistance the most.

A beneficiary has a spendthrift problem

You may want to restrict the compulsive shopper so they can't receive all of their inheritance at one time. You could dictate that they will receive their portion over 5, 10, 15, 20 years or longer. Keep in mind that a lump-sum distribution from your IRA to a beneficiary also means immediate taxation and a big payday for the IRS.

The safest way to make sure your IRA goes to the beneficiaries of your choice is to have your beneficiary forms reviewed annually or when a triggering event occurs.

The Beneficiary Form Trumps All Other Documents

In a ruling on January 26, 2009, on Plan Beneficiary Form in the case of *Kennedy vs. Dupont Savings and Investment Plan*, the U.S. Supreme Court unanimously ruled that William Kennedy's ex-spouse would receive his $402,000 retirement plan because she was the named beneficiary. Mr. Kennedy died in 2001. Under the divorce decree of 1994, his ex-spouse waved her rights to any benefits from his retirement plan. Mr. Kennedy wanted the proceeds to be paid to his daughter. So what could go wrong? Simple, Mr. Kennedy failed to change the beneficiary form. Mr. Kennedy believed because his ex-spouse waived her rights in the divorce decree, he did not need to do anything else. You might ask, why didn't the attorney who handled Mr. Kennedy's divorce advise him to make the appropriate change on his retirement plan's beneficiary form by naming his daughter as primary beneficiary? The answer is simple, like Mr. Kennedy, his attorney believed that because the former Mrs. Kennedy signed the divorce papers, forfeiting any rights to Mr. Kennedy's retirement plan, nothing more needed to be done. This was a $402,000 mistake.

The moral of the story? The beneficiary form is the single most important document in the estate plan. It trumps everything, regardless of what a will, trust, divorce decree or any other signed documents might say!

Here is a list of what to look for to make sure your beneficiary document will get the job done:

1. Do you have a copy?

2. Does it match the copy the Custodian has on file?

3. Does it allow the *"Stretch Option"*?

4. Does it address Simultaneous Death?

5. Are there multiple primary or contingent beneficiaries?

6. Does it automatically establish Separate Accounts?

7. Does it allow for the restriction of a beneficiary?

8. Does it re-direct the IRA proceeds if your beneficiary predeceases you?

9. Does it address beneficiaries under the age of 18?

10. Is it up-to-date?

If it has been a year or longer since the last time you had your beneficiary forms reviewed, it is time to revisit them now. A beneficiary check-up will help you determine whether your beneficiary documents are up-to-date and will accomplish what you want done with your IRAs and other retirement accounts. This simple service will ensure that your family will not have to endure the delay and expense of probate and that the balance of your IRAs and other accounts will go to your intended heirs.

— MISTAKE #4 —
NOT ESTABLISHING SEPARATE ACCOUNTS

The Separate Account Rule dictates that each beneficiary's share must be divided into Separate Accounts. If Separate Accounts with separate beneficiaries are not established, the life expectancy of the oldest beneficiary will apply to all beneficiaries. The deadline to establish Separate Accounts or Separate Contracts is December 31 of the year after the IRA owner's death. The Separate Account Rule is important because multiple beneficiaries will typically have different ages and different life expectancies. Failing to establish Separate Accounts for each beneficiary can be a costly mistake for your younger beneficiaries.

Consider this example of an IRA that is inherited by the owner's daughter and grandson.

John Smith lost his wife three years ago and decided to leave half of his $200,000 IRA to his daughter Shelly, age 45, and the other half to his grandson, Erik, age 12. John filled out the beneficiary form so they would each inherit $100,000. If the beneficiaries had Separate Accounts, Shelly's "*Stretch*" period would be 38.8 years—her remaining life expectancy, according to *IRS Publication 590*. Erik could stretch his distributions over 70.8 years, based on his much longer life expectancy.

Unfortunately the custodian of John's IRA account was not up to speed on the new IRA distribution rules, and when John passed away Separate Accounts were not established. Like many beneficiaries, John's daughter and grandson were not advised about their rights and the importance of establishing Separate Accounts and the December 31 deadline soon passed. As a result, both Shelly and Erik were treated as if they inherited the IRA funds at age 45 and Erik lost the advantage of his much longer life expectancy. Assuming a 5% rate of return, they each will receive approximately $313,000 of income, based on Shelly's 38.8 year life expectancy. For Erik, the total is about a third of what he would have received, had he been able to take the distributions over the *"Stretch"* period based on his life expectancy.

Here is a summary of the scenario:

Without Separate Accounts:
45-year-old inherits $100,000
12-year-old inherits $100,000

Using the same life expectancy - 38.8 years
Daughter age 45 *"Stretch"* income $313,000
Grandson age 12 *"Stretch"* income $313,000

Total distributions to both beneficiaries:
$626,000

DAVID F. ROYER

The 12-year-old beneficiary and the 45-year-old beneficiary were treated as if they were both age 45.

With Separate Accounts:
45-year-old inherits $100,000
12-year-old inherits $100,000

Using individual life expectancies - 38.8 years for Shelly and 70.8 years for Erik
Daughter age 45 *"Stretch"* distributions $313,000
Grandson age 12 *"Stretch"* distributions $945,000

Total distributions to both beneficiaries:
$1,258,000

Erik's *"Stretch"* distributions more than tripled, from $313,000 to $945,000, because Separate Accounts were established. That's because, logically, the longer the inherited IRA distributions can be deferred the longer Erik can continue to earn interest and that will greatly increase his total income from his portion of the inherited IRA. There is typically no cost to establish Separate Accounts, but the cost of not establishing a Separate Account for Erik was $632,000 of lost income.

As mentioned earlier, using a trust to designate multiple beneficiaries could have the same negative effect on the distributions for the younger beneficiaries. *According to IRS Publication 590*:

"The separate account rule cannot be used by the beneficiaries of a trust."

Failing to establish Separate Accounts is a common estate-planning mistake. In many cases, this oversight greatly reduces the value of the *"Stretch Option"* to the younger beneficiaries. The simple solution is to use an IRA beneficiary document that automatically establishes Separate Accounts at the IRA owner's death. These documents should be provided by the custodian of your IRAs and other qualified retirement accounts.

— MISTAKE #5 —
TOO MUCH OF YOUR IRA AT RISK

Albert Einstein once said, *"The most powerful force in the universe is Compound Interest."* This is particularly true when it comes to your IRA, 401(k) and other tax qualified retirement plans. You earn interest on your deposits, you earn interest on your interest and you earn interest on what otherwise would have been paid in taxes in a non-tax-deferred account. **This triple compounding effect can help your retirement accounts grow faster and last longer.**

If you are going to need income from your IRAs or you desire to pass on a legacy of income to your beneficiaries, too much risk can ruin the best made plans.

According to the *Investment Company Fact Book*, published by the Investment Company Institute, approximately 83% of America's pension assets are at risk in the market. By October 2007, the nation's pension assets had grown to a staggering $17.6 trillion. Then the Great Market Crash of 2008 arrived unannounced and many investors' retirement savings evaporated during the worst financial crisis that most Americans have seen in their lifetime.

Before we move further, let's look at a brief overview of the history of turmoil in the U.S. markets. The best place to begin is Black Thursday: October 24, 1929. Odds are, most readers are too young to remember "The Great Market Crash of 1929". Fortunes were lost and by July 1932 the stock market had lost more than 85% of its value. This resulted in massive unemployment, a run on the banks, and America's unemployed workers were standing in soup lines. This also marked the beginning of The Great Depression.

We witnessed similar events during the market crash of 2008 and early 2009. There were no soup lines, however food pantries were stocked to help the poor and those who recently lost their jobs. Unemployment exceeded 10% nationally and was as high as 14% in some states. Although we did not experience a run on the banks, we saw many banks fail, including the Fed seizure of Washington Mutual, representing the biggest bank failure in U.S. history.

Vintage photos from the Depression Era

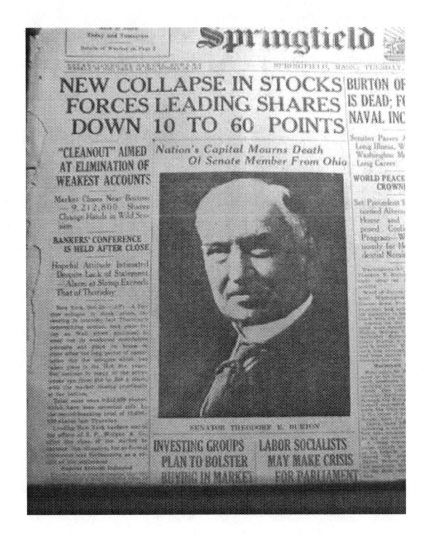

(Franklin D. Roosevelt Library, courtesy of the National Archives and Records Administration.)

(Franklin D. Roosevelt Library, courtesy of the National Archives and Records Administration.)

DAVID F. ROYER

(Franklin D. Roosevelt Library, courtesy of the National Archives and Records Administration.)

Can you see some similarities between the Great Market Crash of 1929 and the more recent Market Crash of 2008? Today all of the windows on Wall Street are sealed to protect innocent pedestrians from desperate Wall Street jumpers.

Fast-forward 55 years to Black Monday: October 19, 1987. This day represented the largest one day drop in the stock market in American history up until that time. Investors lost 22% on equity holdings, amounting to $500 billion in one day.

Then the Tech Stock Crash arrived in March 2000, followed by the terrorist attack on September 11, 2001 (9/11). Both took their toll on the markets and Americans' retirement plans were considerably reduced. After 2002, things started to calm down and investors began to see steady growth in the markets. The S&P 500 grew steadily during the five years between 2002 and 2007 and many investors believed the good times were here to stay.

The years ticked on. Then, without warning, came Grey Tuesday: February 27, 2007. The Dow Jones Industrial Average (DJIA) fell 416 points in one day, the biggest one-day drop since September 17, 2001, the first trading day after 9/11. The U.S. market lost 3.3% in one day because of fears about overvalued China stocks. The headlines the next day blasted the news:

"China Market Plunges, Dow Follows"
— *Chicago Tribune*

"China Volatility Sparks U.S. Sell-Off"
— *USA Today*

"Markets' Slide Spotlights Risk"
—*Wall Street Journal*

This began a critical and devastating turning point in the direction of the market and the American economy.

Just two weeks later, Bad Credit Tuesday arrived on March 13, 2007. The DJIA dropped

242.66 points and the headlines announced a Sub-Prime Lending Meltdown. Remember the ads? No credit, slow credit, bad credit, everyone deserves a mortgage loan. What that meant was borrowers who don't pay their bills should be able to finance homes they cannot afford. Fannie Mae and Freddie Mac were quick to get on board with unsupervised lending and high-risk mortgages. Greed was in the air and everyone was making money, but that would soon come to a very bad end for the American economy.

On September 15, 2008, we witnessed Black Monday, the sequel. The DJIA dropped 504 points. This was the new, biggest one-day drop, beating the tumultuous dip of Grey Tuesday seven months earlier. Lehman Brothers filed for Chapter 11. Banks tightened up credit, and sub-prime lending came to a screeching halt.

The short week between September 15, 2008 and September 19, 2008 was arguably the *most monumental financial crisis since the Great Depression.* Sub-prime lending rocked the financial markets. Lehman Brothers went bankrupt and the Fed seized Washington Mutual. This was the biggest bank failure in American history. On September 29, 2008, lawmakers said no to the $700 billion bailout, causing the DJIA to drop 777.68 points in one day—a loss of $1.2 trillion. Yet another record set for the biggest one-day point drop in American history. Then on October 3, 2008, only four days later, the $700 billion bailout was approved and immediately signed into law, and the DJIA dropped an additional 157.47 points.

Forbes magazine deemed the second week of October 2008, *"The worst week in market history."* The Dow lost 1,873 points in only five days. Many 401(k)s were transformed into 201(k)s. Most IRAs and other qualified accounts took a major beating. The $700 billion bailout had done little to restore confidence in the market and, almost daily, the FDIC added new names to the watch list of banks that could fail. In the automotive industry, Detroit's *"Big Three"* were feeling the pain and looking for bailout money.

On March 10, 2009, Anthony W. Ryan, Assistant Secretary of the U.S. Department of the Treasury, reported, *"The total value of our nation's retirement savings has been estimated at $11 trillion."* That represented a loss of nearly $7 trillion of America's savings and created a financial crisis for retired workers, who were depending on their savings to have a comfortable retirement. Many retired Americans found it necessary to try to rejoin the workforce at a time when unemployment was as high as 10%. Others who were planning to retire were forced to delay their plans.

A week prior to Ryan's comments, on March 2, 2009, the Dow Jones Industrial Average closed under 7,000 points, representing the lowest close in more than 11 years. Then the market began to bounce back. On October 14, 2009, the Dow broke through 10,000 points and on April 13, 2010 it broke through 11,000 points. On February 1, 2011 the Dow closed over 12,000 points, but that was still 15% lower than the highs of 2007. And the roller coaster ride is far from over. We are all hopeful that the market will climb back to its 2007 levels, but the question is:

"Would you bet your life savings that it will happen before you need your money?"

Imagine the number of workers who had plans to retire between 2008 and 2010 but were forced to remain on the job trying to rebuild their IRAs and 401(k) plans. If you had $100,000 invested from January 1, 2000 through December 31, 2010 and your investment performed identically to the S&P 500, you would have only $85,589 left at the end of that 11-year period. If you invested the same $100,000 compounding at only 3% for the same period of time, it would have grown to $138,423 by the end of 2010. That means the Fixed Account, compounding at 3%, would have $52,834 more than the equity account, based on the ups and downs of the S&P 500. The bottom line is that a 0% return would have outperformed the S&P 500 for that 11-year period.

The following chart compares the performance of the S&P 500 vs. a fixed account earning 3% compounded annually. Notice that, although during seven out of eleven years the S&P showed positive growth, the 38.49% loss in 2008 left the S&P account underwater.

Comparison of S&P 500 Performance vs. Fixed Account Earning 3%

YEAR	S&P 500	S&P ACCOUNT*	FIXED ACCOUNT (3%) **
2000	-10.14%	89,860	103,000
2001	-13.04%	78,142	106,090
2002	-23.37%	59,880	109,272
2003	+26.38%	75,676	112,550
2004	+8.99%	82,480	115,927
2005	+3.00%	84,954	119,405
2006	+13.62%	96,525	122,987
2007	+3.53%	99,932	126,677
2008	-38.49%	61,468	130,477
2009	+23.44%	75,877	134,391
2010	+12.80%	$85,589	$138,423

$52,834 More in the Fixed account at only 3%

*Assumes 100% gain or loss based on S&P500
Does not include dividends

**Assumes 3% compounded
Does not include dividends

This chart clearly illustrates the power of compound interest and how easily the Stock Market's ups and downs can have a negative and lasting effect on Americans' retirement accounts. If you had invested $100,000 in both the S&P account and the fixed account, earning 3% during that same 11-year period, which account would you have been more satisfied with at the end of 2010?

I'm not suggesting that the market is a bad choice for everyone or that it's time to hide your money under your mattress. My point is, retired Americans and those planning for retirement will need to depend on their savings to be there when they need it. Having too much of your IRA, 401(k), and other retirement accounts at risk could ruin or delay your retirement plans.

DAVID F. ROYER

Legendary investor Warren Buffett said it best:

Rule #1 "Never lose money!"
Rule #2 "Never forget Rule #1"

Unfortunately the great market crash of 2008 came without warning, and Mr. Buffett's rules became difficult to follow.

In or Out?

When determining how much of your retirement savings to hold in the stock market, the two most important issues to consider are your *time horizon* and *risk tolerance.* Your time horizon is when you will need to take income from your savings to maintain a comfortable retirement. The older you are the shorter your time horizon will be. Calculating your risk tolerance is simple: Don't gamble with more than you can afford to lose.

When considering risk tolerance and time horizon, age is a big factor. A 45-year-old planning to work another 20 years will normally have a greater risk tolerance and a longer time horizon than a 65-year-old retired worker. This makes sense, because the 45-year-old will continue to earn income and can continue to invest in their retirement account for 20-plus more years. The market will go up and down, but over the long haul the market has been proven to grow, and those who are young and still working will normally invest in good or bad market conditions. Their age lets them enjoy the advantages of long-term growth and dollar cost averaging.

Dollar cost averaging is a fundamental strategy to maximize gains, regardless of market conditions. When the market is down, you can buy more shares for the same yearly investment. When the market goes back up, those bargain buys will have a greater value, and can compensate for market losses. This is one of Wall Street's best arguments for keeping your retirement money invested with them.

The 45-year-old investor, in most cases, will not need to tap into their retirement account until their working years are over. Their longer time horizon—the time until they need to spend their retirement money—combined with the advantages of dollar cost averaging make investing in the market attractive.

For the 65-year-old retired person, it's a very different ball game. After retirement many savers are no longer able to contribute to their IRAs and 401(k) plans. They no longer have earned income from their employment, so continued investing may not be an option. The advantage of dollar cost averaging will be lost unless they have earned income and can afford to continue to invest. The other problem facing retired workers is their time horizon is shorter. Social Security and company pensions alone may not produce enough income to keep pace with inflation or to deal with unexpected financial needs. In other words, they may need income from their retirement savings sooner.

DAVID F. ROYER

Even if they still have money to invest, after age 70½ they can no longer contribute to their qualified plans.

(There are exceptions for those over 70½ and still working.)

My point is this:

The best custodian for a retirement plan may be very different for a 45-year-old worker than for a 65-year-old retired person. When you leave the accumulation phase and enter the distribution phase, it's a good time to consider choosing the custodian best suited for the preservation and distribution of your retirement savings.

— MISTAKE #6 —

OVERPAYING FEES AND LOADS ON IRAs, 401(K) AND 403(B) PLANS

The cost of doing business on Wall Street can be more than exposure to risk. The market crash of 2008 and the first quarter of 2009 gave many investors good reason to rethink their approach to a comfortable retirement. For most Americans living today, this was the biggest financial crisis in their lifetime. Now that the market has made a recovery, many investors are looking more closely at the fees and loads that can erode their nest eggs substantially over time.

An article from March 1, 2010, in the *Wall Street Journal*, "The Hidden Costs of Mutual Funds", pointed out doing business on Wall Street can cost investors significantly more than they anticipate. The average expense ratio for mutual funds, according to the article, is 1.31%, but is that the total cost for owning a mutual fund? The hidden costs can be as much as, or in some cases greater than the advertised cost. The buying and selling of securities in the portfolio can add an additional 1% to 3% of undisclosed commission expenses to the owner. Currently the Securities and Exchange Commission does not require these commissions to be factored into the expense ratio, so the average fund owner who thinks they are paying 1-2%, may be paying 3% or more to own a particular fund.

California Congressman George Miller, Chairman of The Committee of Education and Labor, proposed legislation in 2008 that would require full disclosure of hidden fees and loads in 401(k) plans. Wall Street, according to Congressman Miller, opposed the proposed legislation with ferocity.

According to the Investment Company Institute, 83% of American's retirement savings are at risk to market fluctuation and the high fees charged by Wall Street's middlemen. In March 2009, when the DJIA dropped under 7,000—the lowest close in 11 years—all eyes were focused on Wall Street's instability. After two years, and after close to a trillion dollars of taxpayers bailout money was unleashed, on February 1, 2011, the DJIA closed over 12,000 points and IRAs and 401(k) plans saw much awaited growth. Today, retirement savings in America is estimated to be in the $14 trillion range, of which approximately $11.5 trillion is in mutual funds and other securities. Assuming an average of only 2% combined fees and loads, Wall Street will pocket a whopping $230 billion annually of money intended for Americans' retirement years.

A Missed Opportunity

Wall Street's appetite for the fees and loads tied to mutual funds is a lost opportunity for IRA owners. Why a lost opportunity?

"Because fees and loads are out of the compounding formula forever."

The following example illustrates the long-term financial impact of mutual fund fees:

Bob is age 50 and will not need money from his retirement account until he retires at age 65. This means Bob has 15 years of potential growth for his retirement nest egg before he will need income to supplement his Social Security and company pension plan. Let's assume that Bob starts out with $300,000 in retirement savings and that the account will earn 5% compounded interest. Doing the math, $300,000 earning 5% for 15 years will grow to $623,678.

Now let's see what would happen if Bob earned 5% in a mutual fund that charged 2% in fees and loads. The same $300,000 would have grown to only $467,390 in Bob's retirement account by age 65 because the net rate of return would be 3%. That represents a difference of $156,288 less savings at retirement time. The 2% that Bob gave up in fees and loads represented the lost opportunity to earn compound interest. If the total cost of owning the fund averaged 3% to 4%, the negative impact at retirement time would have grown exponentially.

It Doesn't End There!

Fast-forward 15 years, when Bob has reached age 65. He has suffered the loss of $156,288 of savings, due to the loss of compounding of the fees and loads that were systematically extracted from his retirement accounts. Now it's time to begin the distribution phase. The game plan is to transform what is left into a reliable stream of retirement income. This is where the lack of compounding only further compounds the retiree's frustration. As long as Bob's savings remains in his 401(k) or mutual funds, the fees and loads will continue to eat away the potential gains. If there are no gains, the fees and loads will begin to erode the principal.

If Bob needs only 5% annually from his remaining account balance of $467,390, he will still be paying Wall Street its 2%. That will generate a drain of 7% when Bob only needed 5% to maintain his lifestyle in his retirement years. The extra drain due to the cost of doing business with Wall Street is 40% more than Bob needed to reduce his nest egg.

Let's do the math. Bob is now 65 years old, with $467,390 left in his IRA or 401(k). If the account continued to earn 5% and he took only 5% for income, his savings would remain the same ($467,390). But if the account remained under The Street's management, the 2% load would begin to eat away at the principal and the account would be reduced by 2% annually. Wall Street, in this case, is Bob's 40% partner during the distribution phase.

The more the mutual fund owner makes, the more they pay.

If you own a fund with a current value of $500,000 and the total cost of owning that fund is 2%, your annual cost is $10,000. This money is unceremoniously removed from the IRA owner's account each year. In the above scenario, assume that Bob's account has grown from $500,000 to $600,000 after several years of market gains. The same 2% load will have gone from $10,000 to $12,000.

Try to visualize someone reaching into your retirement savings and removing $10,000 or more each year. Next imagine that same person using that money to take a lavish vacation or buy an expensive watch. At this point you might say, *"They can't do that!"* Unfortunately they *can* do that, and that is exactly what they *are* doing.

The Solution:

Get help to uncover the hidden costs of owning your mutual funds. Look beyond the expense ratio and dig into the turnover ratio and other hidden trading and advertising expenses.

Understand how these fees, loads and other expenses are taken out of your accounts each year. Consequently less than 100% of your money is working for you.

Also, understand the long-term effect due to the lack of compounding interest on the money that has been removed from your accounts. Calculate how the fees and loads will impact your retirement income or could reduce the inheritance to your heirs.

The End Result:

You may be comfortable with the cost of owning a particular fund, or you may have just gone into shock after learning about the hidden fees and loads. The key issue is that if you are aware of the real cost of owning a particular fund, you can make informed decisions about positioning your retirement assets.

The current turbulence on Wall Street and the high cost of investing in mutual funds are reason enough for anyone to reassess their investment choices, reduce expenses, and take the appropriate steps to guarantee a comfortable and risk-free retirement.

— MISTAKE #7 —

NOT TAKING ADVANTAGE OF TAX SAVING STRATEGIES

Two strategies can transform taxable IRAs into tax-free income or a tax-free inheritance. You have the option to pay the tax on the seed now and save the tax on the crop when it comes time to harvest some of your retirement savings. For many owners of qualified retirement plans, the Roth IRA Conversion or IRA Arbitrage can offer an effective way to fire the IRS and take full control of your retirement accounts.

The Roth IRA Conversion

Never pay income tax before you have to. Sound familiar? This was a good strategy for most people until the Roth IRA was born on January 1, 1998, as a result of the Taxpayer Relief Act of 1997. The Roth concept is simple: You don't get a tax deduction when you make a contribution to your Roth IRA, but future growth and distributions are income tax free. For those with traditional IRAs, 401(k)s, 403(b)s, SEPs, and other qualified retirement plans, future growth and distributions are fully taxable. You have the option to convert these plans to a tax-free Roth IRA. The Roth IRA

Conversion offers an opportunity to pay the income tax now and have your nest egg grow free from income tax, and qualified distributions can be taken income tax free. Until recently, the Roth Conversion was only available to those who had joint or single incomes of less than $100,000. Effective January 1, 2010, under the Pension Protection Act, all IRA owners, including those with incomes over $100,000, can take advantage of the Roth IRA Conversion.

You can choose to convert all or a portion of your IRA to a Roth IRA. If you choose to convert to a Roth IRA, you will owe income tax, both federal and state, on the amount you converted. For example, if you convert a $100,000 IRA to a Roth IRA, and your combined federal and state income tax is 30%, you will owe $30,000 in total conversion taxes.

It may seem counterintuitive, but converting a traditional IRA or other qualified retirement plan to a Roth IRA is one of the best strategies to protect your retirement assets from excessive taxation. From the moment you made your first contribution to your qualified retirement plans, Uncle Sam became your partner. The unfortunate aspect about this partnership is that after you take all of the investment risk, Uncle Sam can determine what percentage of your retirement account belongs to him. This is done simply by raising income tax brackets. Converting your traditional plans to a Roth IRA can sever your unwanted partnership with the fewest dollars possible. It's a way to take full ownership of your retirement savings.

Of course, the only way out of an IRA is through the IRS—and Uncle Sam is going to hold you to your original agreement. Under the traditional IRA, your contributions were not taxed, but all of the gains and future distributions are fully taxable. You saved the tax on the seed, but when it comes time to harvest that hard-earned savings, you must pay the tax on the crop. Although you will have to pay that tax bill now if you convert your account to Roth IRA, you likely will pay less now in taxes than if you wait another 5, 10 or 15 years. If your IRS partner chooses to raise the tax rates—which most economists agree is just over the horizon—the long-term tax implications for your retirement savings could be substantially more than what you will pay if you convert to a Roth now. Because the Bush Era tax cuts have been extended through 2012, you have an opportunity to convert to the Roth IRA while there is still an income tax sale.

The Roth Conversion will be most effective for IRA owners who won't need income from their IRAs, and who desire to pass more on to their heirs and eliminate the income tax. After converting to a Roth IRA, the owner and surviving spouse are no longer forced to take required distributions after turning age 70½. Think of the advantage for the children and grandchildren. The account is still earning interest but there are no required distributions, so the Roth account grows faster. When distributions are finally taken, they are income tax free! There is a special gold nugget in the tax code for those who take advantage of the Roth IRA Conversion. After the conversion, the Roth IRA can be structured to take advantage of the *"Stretch Option".* Your heirs will be able to enjoy a lifetime of income and all of the *"Stretch"* distributions will be income tax free!

Five-Year Holding Period

There is a five-year holding period after a Roth Conversion. If any distributions taken within the five-year holding period include investment earnings, taxes must be paid on the earnings only. The amount that was originally converted to the Roth IRA can be withdrawn, income tax free, even during the five-year holding period. For example, if you convert a $200,000 IRA to a Roth IRA you can take a tax free withdrawal of up to $200,000, during the five-year holding period, income tax free.

Required Minimum Distribution in the Year of Conversion

If you are age 70½ or older when you convert to a Roth IRA, the Required Minimum Distribution for the current year must be taken prior to the Roth Conversion.

Example Age 79:

$500,000	IRA Balance as of December 31
- $26,650	Current Year's RMD (5.13%)
$473,350	Eligible to Convert to a Roth IRA

In this same example, if you were less than age 70½, you would have been able to convert the entire $500,000 to a Roth IRA.

Before you convert your traditional IRA to the Roth IRA, you should be aware of some important considerations. The Roth IRA Conversion can be very attractive to some IRA owners and a big mistake for others.

5 Signs that You May Be a Good Candidate for the Roth IRA Conversion:

1. You are 59½ or older and do not plan to take distributions within five years after the conversion.

2. You expect to live long enough to recoup the conversion tax. If you convert a $300,000 IRA to a Roth IRA and pay 33% total tax, the cost of the conversion will be $99,000. How long will it take, at a reasonable rate of return, to earn back the conversion tax inside the Roth IRA?

3. You have non-qualified funds to pay the conversion tax. Paying the conversion tax out of the IRA will mean less money in the new Roth growing income tax free and less tax-free income. Paying the conversion tax with non-IRA money means you can leave more money in your Roth IRA and leave a larger nest egg to your beneficiaries, free of any income tax.

4. You believe your tax bracket or your surviving heir's tax brackets will be higher in the future. Ask yourself this question: *do you think income tax rates are more likely to go up or down?* If you think you, or your heirs, will be in a higher tax bracket than you are in today, the Roth IRA Conversion makes sense.

5. Your goal is to pass more money to your heirs, income tax free. One of the greatest benefits of the Roth IRA Conversion is using it as a wealth transfer tool. Your children and grandchildren can enjoy a lifetime of tax-free income. That puts the IRS completely out of the picture.

5 Signs that You Are <u>Not</u> a Good Candidate for the Roth IRA Conversion:

1. You are under age 59½ and will need to take distributions within five years after conversion. You will pay an additional 10% penalty for any distributions taken prior to turning age 59½.

2. You are at an advanced age or in poor health and you are not likely to recoup the conversion tax.

3. The conversion tax will need to be paid out of the IRA and you are younger than 59½. The portion of the IRA that is used to pay conversion taxes will generate a 10% pre-59½ penalty. Even

though that portion is going to the IRS, it is still considered a pre-59½ withdrawal.

4. You believe your tax bracket will be similar or lower in the future. This is a sure sign not to convert. Why pay a higher tax rate to convert than you would pay if you simply took your required distributions?

5. The conversion will raise your marginal tax bracket. When you convert, the amount converted is considered income and could push you into a higher tax bracket, making it less attractive to move your retirement savings into a Roth IRA. In this case, a partial conversion would make more sense. Convert only the amount that will keep you in a reasonable tax bracket.

The Roth Conversion Safety Net

After converting to a Roth IRA you can change your mind. You will have until October 15 of the following year to change the Roth IRA back to a traditional IRA to avoid paying the conversion tax. This process is called *recharacterization*. It is an important tax saving maneuver if the account loses value after converting to a Roth.

For example, if Jane decided to convert her $300,000 IRA to a Roth IRA and she is in a 40% combined federal and state income tax bracket, the conversion tax would be $120,000 ($300,000 × 40% tax bracket = $120,000 of conversion taxes).

If after the conversion her account lost money and the account value dropped to $200,000, she would still owe the tax on the original $300,000 that she converted. The best solution, for Jane, might be to recharacterize back to a traditional IRA and eliminate the conversion tax. If Jane missed the October 15 deadline to recharacterize, she will have missed the opportunity to save a substantial portion of the conversion taxes.

Re-conversion to a Roth IRA

If you decide to recharacterize the Roth back to a traditional IRA to avoid paying an inflated conversion tax, you are allowed to convert to a Roth IRA again. In Jane's case, she would be able to convert the reduced amount of $200,000 to a Roth IRA and the conversion tax would be only $80,000 *($200,000 × her 40% tax bracket = $80,000 of conversion taxes)*. Jane would have saved $40,000 in conversion taxes, using this strategy.

There is one rule; you cannot re-convert in the same year you chose to recharacterize or within 30 days after you recharacterized.

IRA Arbitrage

IRA Arbitrage is nothing more than converting your IRA into life insurance. You might ask, why would anyone want to pay the tax on their IRA and put what is left into life insurance? The answer is that it can be a smart estate-planning move.

Many IRA owners are affluent and will not need much, if any, of their IRA funds to produce post-retirement income. For these owners, IRA Arbitrage may be the best way to pass more tax-free dollars to the next generation.

Consider the retired engineer who has a defined benefit pension plan that will provide him with $160,000 annually for life, or the retired physician who has saved money in an SEP/IRA and sold his practice for $2 million. Will either of these IRA owners need their IRAs to provide income for their retirement years?

One solution for those who have this type of financial security is to use the after-tax value of their IRA to purchase life insurance. Life insurance will typically increase the money left to the heirs and eliminate the income tax.

5 Strategies for IRA Arbitrage:

1. **Cash out the IRA and purchase a single premium life insurance policy**. The following chart is an example of a 65-year-old male who owns a $300,000 IRA and will pay a total of 40% in taxes to cash it out. $120,000 (40%) will go to taxes and $180,000 (60%) will be left to purchase a single premium life insurance policy. Assuming the owner is in reasonably good health, the $180,000 left after paying the IRA taxes would be enough money to generate a $400,000 income tax-free death benefit using life insurance. If he kept his money in the IRA,

the after-tax death benefit to the heirs would be $180,000, at age 65, increasing to $235,294 by age 85, assuming the account is growing at 5% and the IRA owner withdraws only his Required Minimum Distributions. Purchasing a life insurance policy, in this case, will increase the after-tax benefit to the heirs by $220,000 *($400k life insurance-$180,000 after-tax IRA = $220,000 more for the beneficiaries).* By age 85 the total life insurance benefit to the heirs would have grown to more than $670,000, income tax free.

The following chart illustrates the difference in the after tax inheritance between keeping the IRA or cashing it out and putting the after tax money into a single-premium life insurance. Assuming the IRA owner is age 65 when the life insurance is purchased, it compares the benefits to the beneficiaries at age 65, 75, and 85.

IRA vs. Single Premium Life Insurance
$300,000 IRA — 40% Combined Tax to Heirs

Age	IRA Value*	Cum RMD	Income Tax	Net to Heirs	Life Premium	Net to Heirs
65	$300,000	$0	$120,000	$180,000	$180,000	$400,000**
75	$415,349	$83,119	$166,140	$249,209	$0	$400,000**
85	$392,157	$310,269	$156,863	$235,294	$0	$672,692**

Life Insurance Doubled the After Tax Benefit to the Heirs

*5% Rate of Return   **Indexed UL 6.9% Return Less Insurance Charges

DAVID F. ROYER

2. **Use a combination approach with Roth IRA Arbitrage**. This strategy uses life insurance to pay the Roth IRA conversion tax after the IRA owner's death. For example, assume Robert has a traditional IRA valued at $1,000,000 and the conversion tax is estimated to be 35%, or $350,000, and he does not have sufficient liquidity to pay the conversion tax. A more affordable option would be to purchase a $350,000 life insurance policy and use the tax-free proceeds to pay the conversion tax at death. Robert's surviving spouse will have tax-free money to pay the conversion tax and would then own a $1 million tax-free Roth IRA. The spouse will then be able to pass a lifetime of tax free income to the children and grandchildren, using the "Stretch Option".

3. **Use the IRA value to purchase a 7 Pay life insurance policy.** This will spread the distribution tax over seven years and may help the owner remain in a lower tax bracket.

4. **Use after-tax RMDs to purchase life insurance**. If the IRA owner doesn't need the required distributions for income purposes, they can be used to pay ongoing life insurance premiums and increase the tax-free benefits to the beneficiaries.

5. **Use annual withdrawals from an IRA Annuity to purchase life insurance**. Most annuities have a 10% free withdrawal feature that can be used every year. The free withdrawal feature can be used to purchase tax-free life

insurance. This is an effective strategy for those wanting to leave an income tax free legacy for their spouses, children/grandchildren, or other beneficiaries.

All five approaches to converting IRAs to life insurance have the potential to increase the inheritance and eliminate the income taxes for the IRA owner's heirs. Best of all, you will have fired your unwanted partner, Uncle Sam, with the fewest dollars possible and prevented the IRS from becoming the senior partner in your retirement plan.

5 Additional Advantages of Life Insurance:

1. **Access to Cash Values** – Your premium is not gone; it is now in the form of life insurance cash values that you can access when you need some of your money for income or unexpected expenses.

2. **Income Tax Advantages** – Permanent life insurance offers three major income tax advantages: tax-deferred build-up of cash values, tax-free access to the cash values via low net interest loans, and tax-free death benefits for the beneficiaries. Think of the advantages for the life insurance owner and their beneficiaries. The cash value grows tax deferred and can provide the owner a steady stream of tax-free retirement income and, at the owner's death, the beneficiaries will receive a

tax-free death benefit. Here is the best part. When you borrow from a life insurance policy you will pay only a small net loan interest because you will continue to earn interest on the borrowed amount. If you take a loan from a life insurance policy that is earning 5% interest and the loan interest rate is 6%, you will only pay a net 1% interest on the borrowed amount.

Example:

Jack borrowed $10,000 from his life insurance policy to supplement his retirement income. The policy has a 6% loan interest rate so he would owe $600 of loan interest. However Jack is being credited 5% ($500) on the borrowed amount. Consequently his net loan interest rate is only 1% ($100). Jack pays no income tax because this is considered a loan rather than a taxable withdrawal. If Jack withdrew the same $10,000 from any other interest bearing account, he would pay income tax on the interest withdrawn. In this case, the cost of using the cash value of his life insurance is only 1% as compared to as much as 35% if he were forced to pay income tax.

Now for the icing on the cake, Jack will never need to repay the loan. One reason is that the cash value already belongs to Jack, so he is borrowing his own money and doing so tax free. The second reason is the death benefit

will pay the loan off when Jack is gone.
For many, just like Jack, life insurance can be
the most tax advantaged retirement plan
imaginable.

With tax increases just over the short-term
horizon, the unique tax advantages of permanent life insurance are gaining increased
importance.

3. **Nursing Home Waiver** – This feature is available with some carriers and eliminates future
premiums in the event you are confined to a
nursing home.

4. **Terminal Illness Riders** – This benefit allows
you to withdrawal some or all of the death benefit if you are diagnosed as being terminally ill and
death is expected within one year.

5. **Long-Term Care Riders** – This is a tremendous
benefit for those who don't own Long-Term Care
insurance and is available with some carriers.
Using the life insurance benefit to fund Long-
Term Care expenses eliminates the need to pay
large annual Long-Term Care premiums.
Approximately 85% of Americans over age 65
have no Long-Term Care insurance, and it is estimated that 60% of us will incur some Long-Term
Care expenses. In 2010, the average annual cost
of nursing home care was close to $70,000.
Imagine how quickly your retirement savings
can be depleted if you or your spouse have need

for care. These Long-Term Care riders offered by some life insurance contracts can be a cost-effective way to prevent your life savings from being spent on nursing home expenses.

The Roth IRA Conversion and IRA Arbitrage can put you back in control of your IRAs and other retirement accounts. Both strategies let you, as the owner, determine when the IRA taxes will be paid and also offer some control over what the tax rates will be.

DAVID F. ROYER

— MISTAKE #8 —

NOT ROLLING 401(K) OR 403(B) PLANS TO AN IRA

Participating in a company-sponsored 401(k) or 403(b) plan has long been viewed as the best game in town for two reasons:

1. Contributions were not taxed and are deducted directly from your paycheck, so you hardly miss the money.

2. Most plans offer company matching funds, some as high as 100% of the employee's contribution. What could beat that? You double your money up front!

For many retired workers, their 401(k) plans represent the majority of their retirement savings, and for some, their 401(k) is worth more than their home. However, after retirement both reasons to remain in the 401(k) or 403(b) are gone forever. You can no longer make tax-deductible contributions and there are no longer company matching funds. Now is a good time to roll the 401(k) or 403(b) to a more flexible IRA and take control of your retirement savings.

5 Good Reasons to Move Your 401(k) or 403(b) When You Retire:

1. **Most 401(k)s, 403(b)s and other company plans have limited investment options.** They may offer 50 different mutual funds and other investment vehicles, but most of the options are subject to market fluctuations. If we learned anything in 2008 and early 2009, it was that what the market gives gradually can be taken away quickly with little to no warning. Many company plans lost as much as 40% in 2008 alone. Those individuals who chose to play it safe and moved their 401(k) money into bond funds or funds invested in CDs and other short-term investments were rewarded with little or no growth, while inflation and management fees ate away at their principal. Moving the 401(k) or 403(b) to an IRA will offer the owner unlimited investment options. Some of these options can guarantee the principal, offer a competitive rate of return, and generate an income that cannot be outlived.

2. **Plan guidelines can restrict the owner's access to their money.** The plan document is essentially the 401(k) rulebook. If it is not in the book, you can't do it! With savings down and unemployment up, you never know when you may need access to your retirement accounts. IRAs offer greater flexibility, allowing the owners to make their own rules if they are willing to pay the tax on the distributions.

3. **Direct rollovers avoid the 20% mandatory withholding**. It's critical that the funds are moved as a trustee-to-trustee transfer. If a check is written to the 401(k) owner, you can count on the custodian withholding 20% for the IRS. I have worked with several financial planners who have encountered this problem, and they are still battling with the IRS to get the 20% withholding back where it belongs.

4. **401(k) and 403(b) plans have limited distribution flexibility for the children and grandchildren, who are likely to inherit when both the owner and spouse are gone**. In 2002, when the *"Stretch Option"* was born, children and grandchildren of IRA owners were given new valuable distribution options. They now have the ability to spread the inherited IRA distributions over their individual life expectancies, according to Appendix C, Table 1 of *IRS Publication 590*. This means they are no longer forced into rapid distribution, causing rapid taxation. Unfortunately most 401(k) plan administrators didn't get on board with this valuable income planning tool and, in many cases, they are forcing these non-spousal beneficiaries to take full taxable distribution in just five years. Under the Worker, Retiree and Employer Recovery Act of 2008 (HR 7327), beginning January 1, 2010, all employer plans were required to allow non-spousal beneficiaries to do direct rollovers to inherited IRAs. Rolling the inherited company plan to an IRA allows

these beneficiaries to take control of their inheritance and opens up unlimited investment options and greater income flexibility.

5. **Most 401(k) and 403(b) plans do not allow the Roth IRA Conversion**. New legislation, The Small Business Jobs Act of 2010, now allows 401(k) participants to roll their traditional 401(k) to a Roth 401(k); however, until their plan documents are amended, most plans will not permit this maneuver. Beginning in 2010, IRA owners with adjusted gross incomes over $100,000 could, for the first time, convert their traditional IRAs to the Roth IRA. After the conversion tax is paid, the new Roth will grow income tax free, and distributions after the five-year holding period will also be income tax free. The Pension Protection Act simplified Roth Conversions from 401(k)s and other company sponsored plans. Beginning in 2008, owners could convert company sponsored plans directly to a Roth IRA. They no longer needed to convert to a traditional IRA before converting to a Roth IRA.

The good news is that you may not have to wait until you retire to move your 401(k) or 403(b) plan to an IRA.

Approximately 70% of 401(k) plans allow for an In-Service Transfer. That means there is a 70% chance you can move the 401(k) to an IRA while you are still working, making contributions, and enjoying company matching funds. Most of the plans that allow the transfer require the employee to be at least age 59½. You will need to check with your plan administrator or your HR department to see whether your plan allows for the In-Service Transfer. You should also make sure that there is no blackout period. A blackout period is a period of time after making the transfer that you may not be able to continue to make contributions or receive company-matching funds.

There is a special gold nugget in the tax code for those who are employees or retired employees of non-profit organizations, such as hospitals, museums, public foundations, churches, research organizations, or public educational systems, and who made contributions to their 403(b) or Tax-Sheltered Annuity (TSA) plans.

Most 403(b) plans and TSAs allow the owners to switch to an IRA if they are over 59½, have a break in service, or transfer to a new school district. In our current economic environment, many educators are being forced into early retirement. This is another opportunity to move their restrictive 403(b) plans and other teachers' retirement plans to a more flexible IRA.

If you currently have a 401(k), 403(b) or other company-sponsored plan, you should examine all of your options to decide whether rolling the plan to the more flexible IRA is consistent with your overall retirement goals.

— MISTAKE #9 —
TOO MANY
RETIREMENT ACCOUNTS

People saving for their retirement years commonly find themselves with more accounts than they know what to do with. How does this happen? Throughout our working years, we have sporadic opportunities to save for retirement and we are told diversification is the key to retirement success. As a result many savers find themselves with multiple retirement accounts; for example, three CDs, a Money Market Account, two annuities, an IRA, a 401(k) or 403(b), and two brokerage accounts. That would be a total of 10 separate retirement accounts and for some, this can be retirement mess.

Having too many retirement accounts is a high-quality problem, but a problem nonetheless. When it is time to convert some of your savings into an income stream, several important considerations must be taken into account.

Here are just a few challenges caused by having too many retirement accounts:

Determining which account you should spend first and how you should withdraw the money

When the time comes to use some of your savings to supplement your retirement income, the more retirement accounts you own, the more difficult it will be to make good choices. One of the biggest and most common retirement mistakes is withdrawing the interest only from your non-qualified CDs, annuities, Money Market accounts, and other interest bearing accounts. Taking the interest only may seem like a good idea, because you will still have your entire principal. The problem is that all of the interest you withdraw will be considered taxable income. With CDs and Money Market accounts, the interest is currently taxable whether or not you take it out. Your non-qualified savings accounts can be consolidated into one tax-deferred account that will only be taxed when you choose to withdraw some of your interest earnings. These types of accounts, with few exceptions, use the *"Last in First out Rule"*. This means when you choose to take withdrawals, they will be considered taxable interest until the entire amount of your interest earnings has been removed. The advantage of tax deferral is you can decide when the tax is due by making withdrawals when it best fits your plans.

Controlling your taxable income after retirement has additional tax benefits. The more taxable income you have, the more likely you will find yourself in a higher tax bracket. If your taxable income exceeds the Social Security income limit, you may be forced to pay income tax on up to 85% of your Social Security benefits. Choosing the right account will be less of a challenge if you consolidate some accounts and use income strategies that will lower your overall tax bill.

Determining how to calculate Required Minimum Distributions from multiple qualified accounts

This can be tricky if you own more than one type of retirement account. For example, you may own an IRA, a 401(k), and a 403(b) plan. That would be three different types of qualified retirement plans. In Mistake #1 we discussed the importance of taking Required Minimum Distributions after turning age 70½. Let's assume that each of your three plans has a balance of $100,000. That comes to a combined total of $300,000. To keep the math simple, let's assume your RMD for the current year is 5%. You will need to take a total distribution of $15,000 ($5,000 per account) for the current year's RMD. *You must take the required amount from each of the three accounts.* In other words, you cannot take $15,000 from just one account to satisfy the RMD for all three accounts, even though the total distribution would be the same either way. If all three accounts were IRAs, you would then have the option to choose the account from which you take your RMD. You could choose to take the entire $15,000 from one of the accounts allowing the others to continue to grow tax-deferred. You can also choose to roll the 401(k) and 403(b) into your IRA and then you would only need to manage one qualified retirement account. If you are retired and still have some of your money in a 401(k) or other company sponsored plan, it's time to roll the plan to an IRA. This will give you greater flexibility and simplify your choices when it's time to take your Required Minimum Distributions. The more retirement plans you own, the greater your chance of making costly retirement mistakes.

Determining whether you will have enough money for a comfortable retirement

This is a big concern for those who are not fortunate enough to have retirement income from a company-sponsored retirement plan. Consider the retired worker who has a Defined Benefit Pension Plan and will receive more than $100,000 a year for life. Unfortunately, the days of the big company pension plans are all but gone. As these types of plans continue to disappear, each year more retiring Americans will need to depend on their IRAs, 401(k)s and other plans to supplement their Social Security. Having these accounts spread all over the place just compounds the problem. Before determining the amount of income you can take from your savings, you need to know how much you have in these accounts. Some accounts may be growing, while others are shrinking. These fluctuating account balances need to be taken into consideration when making income decisions. If you take too much income to fast, you run the risk of running out of income during your retirement years. When the account is empty, the income from that account will stop. Consolidating your accounts can simplify this process and make income decisions less of a task.

Determining whether your beneficiaries are up-to-date on all of your retirement accounts

In Mistake #3 we discussed the many tax traps that IRA owners must navigate when properly setting up beneficiaries. If you have only one IRA, it is difficult enough to get everything set up properly to avoid costly mistakes that can result in accelerated taxes and beneficiaries losing the advantages of the *"Stretch Option"*. Even worse, your retirement savings could end up in the hands of an ex-spouse or ex-son/daughter-in-law if your beneficiary forms are not kept up-to-date. If you have 10 retirement accounts, the chance of making costly beneficiary mistakes is multiplied tenfold!

Determining what to do with old life insurance policies

Consolidation also can be beneficial in the area of life insurance. Statistics show that Americans commonly own three or more life insurance policies. Most people nearing retirement bought life insurance when they were young and still raising their families. The purpose of life insurance, at that time, was to provide income for the family if they died prematurely. If you are reading this and your children are grown and on their own, that reason is gone.

For many people, the cash values of their life insurance policies have grown to the point that they are substantial nest eggs. This can represent a golden opportunity. In many cases, the cash value of your life insurance may be very close to the death benefit. For example, if you bought a whole life policy 20 or 30 years ago with a $100,000 death benefit and the cash value has now grown to $70,000, the net death benefit is only $30,000 *($100,000 death benefit minus the $70,000 that already belongs to you)*. People are living longer, and the cost of life insurance has decreased. You are allowed to do a tax free exchange of your $70,000 cash value to a new life insurance policy, and that could increase your death benefit from a net of $30,000 to as much as $200,000, depending on your age and health. The death benefit will be greater and it will be paid income tax free to your beneficiaries. This is a huge gold nugget in the tax code.

If you have several old life insurance policies, they can all be consolidated into one larger policy. Here is the best part: when you do this, in most cases, you will no longer need to pay life insurance premiums. The new policy will have cash values, just like the current policies. These cash values can be used for emergencies, to provide retirement income, or for any other purpose. If you need to make a beneficiary change, you only have to do it once. This decreases the chance of making beneficiary mistakes.

Simplification through Consolidation

Having too many accounts is just too much to worry about, but there is a simple solution. Multiple retirement accounts can be consolidated into two basic categories: Qualified and Non-Qualified.

Qualified accounts include IRAs, 401(k)s, 403(b)s, 457(b)s, SEPs, and similar accounts where you did not pay income tax on your contributions. All of these qualified accounts can be consolidated into one easily managed IRA. The Non-Qualified category includes everything else. Many retired workers, or those planning to retire, can consolidate multiple accounts into two easily managed retirement accounts *(and a third account for those who own a Roth IRA)*.

If you choose to consolidate some of your retirement accounts to make life a little simpler, you will need to consider how you will transfer funds from one account to another. There are two methods of transferring retirement accounts, and there are different rules for each.

1. Trustee to Trustee Transfer

This is the safest way to transfer your retirement accounts. Using this method, the funds are moved directly from the current financial institution to the new one that you choose. You simply complete the transfer request and the rest is on autopilot. You will not receive a check or need to create a paper trail to prove to the IRS that this is a transfer and not a taxable distribution. Another advantage is you can make these types of transfers as often as you like, so if you change your mind you can transfer your savings somewhere else. This method may take a little more time, usually 20 to 45 days, but you don't run the risk of needing to prove that the transfer did not trigger a taxable event.

2. IRA Rollover

This method is faster, but there are two major tax traps. When doing an IRA rollover, the current custodian will send you a check and you must reinvest the funds into a new IRA within 60 days. If you pass the 60 day deadline and fail to reinvest the money into a new IRA, the IRS will have a hit a home run, with the bases loaded. The funds will lose their tax-deferred status and will become taxable immediately. The second tax trap is that you may only do one rollover per IRA in a 12-month period. If you do more than one rollover with the same

IRA during the 12-month waiting period, the IRA will become taxable. If after completing an IRA rollover, you decide to move your IRA again, the only safe option will be to do a trustee to trustee transfer, or wait until the 12 months have passed.

Here are two examples of how easily you can step into these tax traps:

Tax Trap 1 – The 60 Day Limit

Jim, age 63, owned a $200,000 IRA in a brokerage account. He had lost a little over $8,000 in the past year and was ready to take an early retirement. He decided he had lost enough and he initiated an IRA rollover. His plan was to move the account to a bank CD to keep his money safe. He received the check from the brokerage firm on March 1, 2008, so he had until April 30, 2008 *(60 days later)* to deposit his IRA at the bank.

On March 19 Jim retired from his company and he and his wife took a long and well-deserved vacation. When they returned from vacation, three weeks later, Jim's wife began to have some health issues and he was focused on getting her the best care available. The 60-day deadline to reinvest his IRA had passed unnoticed, and the tax trap was triggered. Jim's entire $200,000 IRA became taxable.

Tax Trap 2 – One Rollover per IRA per Year

Elizabeth, a widow age 66, was married to a very conservative investor who believed in one motto, *"Never take chances with money."* His $400,000 IRA was in a money market account that was paying a low interest rate. The money was safe, but the earnings were poor. Elizabeth had always been more of a risk taker than her husband and, many times, she encouraged him to take a little more risk to increase the potential earnings. After her husband's death, Elizabeth chose to become the new IRA owner. The stage was set and she was ready to reposition the IRA for better growth. At that time the six-month bank CD interest rates were much higher than her money market account, so she instructed the financial institution to send her a check for the entire $400,000, which she deposited into the CD within the 60 day limit. Elizabeth was pleased with her decision.

Several months later, a friend told Elizabeth that she had earned more than 14% in a mutual fund last year. That is the kind of growth Elizabeth was looking for. After the six-month CD matured, Elizabeth went to the bank and withdrew the CD, placing the money in the mutual fund, again within the 60-day limit. What did Elizabeth do wrong? She made two IRA rollovers from the same IRA within the 12 month period and triggered a tax trap. Elizabeth now owed income tax on the entire $400,000.

As bad as both of these tax traps are, they could have been much worse. If Jim in tax trap 1, or Elizabeth in tax trap 2, were under age 59½, they would have paid an additional 10% penalty for taking a pre-59½ distribution from their IRAs. For Elizabeth, who was 66, the additional taxable income generated from her IRA mistake would easily be sufficient to push her into a higher tax bracket and increase the tax on her Social Security benefits.

IRA mistakes are easy to make with only one account. If you own multiple retirement accounts, the chance of triggering an unwanted taxable event is significantly increased.

For many years, financial pundits have touted the maxim that diversification is the best way to prepare for retirement. *"Don't put all of your eggs in the same basket."* During the accumulation years, that made perfectly good sense; however, when you decide to retire, diversification needs to give way to preservation. It's all about having enough income for a comfortable retirement. Here is the simple truth: ***You cannot have a guaranteed income from a non-guaranteed account!*** A drop in the market, like we saw in 2008, for many retirees can mean reduced retirement income. Consolidating retirement accounts in a safe place can help avoid costly and irreversible retirement mistakes.

— MISTAKE #10 —

NOT GETTING A SECOND OPINION

Failure to seek counsel from a second source is the granddaddy of all retirement planning mistakes. It is how many investors and retirees find themselves taking financial losses, and paying unnecessary taxes, penalties, fees and loads. The IRA owner's worst enemy is bad advice offered by the unskilled and untrained advisor. Getting a second opinion regarding your wealth is equally as critical as getting a second opinion about your health.

Imagine during a routine checkup your family doctor discovers something doesn't sound quite right with your heart. How would you feel if he said, *"Make an appointment with my nurse to come in next week for open heart surgery."* You might faint at the thought of a family practitioner wanting to perform a surgery he or she has no training to perform. The doctor is more likely to recommend that you visit a cardiologist to get a second opinion before anyone pulls out the chest cutter. This process is designed to get you to the right professional who is trained to perform the needed procedure.

In the financial services industry, finding that right professional to give you a second opinion can be a bit tricky. The reality is that the fees, loads and commissions associated with managing the trillions of dollars of Americans' retirement savings is big business. You can be sure that most advisors have no intention of referring you to an IRA distribution specialist. They will not run the risk of losing your account, even if it is in your best interest to make the referral.

Before choosing an advisor to get a second opinion, understand that most advisors are not trained in the complex arena of IRA distribution planning. Consider the Property and Casualty agent who spends his days sending out thousands of mailers offering to save you 25% on your auto or home owners insurance, or the stock broker who left you drowning in the market in 2008. Are these advisors likely to be qualified to advise you in IRA or 401(k) planning? As with open heart surgery, you want to find the right advisor for the job. To accomplish this, you should first understand the different types of financial professionals you may encounter.

7 Basic Categories of Consumer Advisors:

1. **Bank Advisors** – Most of us have some experience with banks. We use them for checking accounts, savings accounts, loans and credit cards. Usually, when you choose to save money in a bank, your money will wind up in a CD,

Money Market account, or other bank product. Bank employees are trained to advise you to put your IRA in a CD or other bank product, because that is what they sell. They will assure you that your retirement funds will be safe. However, although CDs and Money Market accounts are generally considered safe, the trade-off for safety is typically a lower rate of return.

Similarly, they will assure you that you will get a fair rate of return—but a fair rate of return may not be enough when you're taking Required Minimum Distributions from your IRA. When you turn 70½ your first required distribution is 3.65% of the IRA account balance as of December 31 of the prior year. If the CD is earning less than 3.65%, your IRA will begin to shrink. As you get older, the required distribution percentages will increase. At age 75, it's 4.37% and at age 80, it's 5.35% of the account balance as of December 31 of the prior year. If the CD rate is consistently lower than the Required Minimum Distribution, your IRA will shrink fast and there will be less (if any) money left in your IRA to be passed on to your heirs. Bank advisors, with very few exceptions, are not trained in the IRA distribution rules and are not in a position to help you develop winning IRA strategies.

Moreover, in 2008 we learned that banks are not always financially sound and many banks were involved in high risk mortgage loans. As a result of banks granting loans to consumers with bad credit or even no credit, nearly 30 banks failed in 2008, leading the federal government to take action. On September 25, 2008, the Fed seized Washington Mutual. This was the biggest bank failure in American history. Congress swiftly passed legislation to provide billions of dollars in "bailout" money to other ailing banks to keep them from turning upside-down. Despite the government's involvement, however, things continued to fall apart for the next two years. In 2009, more than 140 banks failed, and more than 200 failed in 2010. A big chunk of the bailout money went to big banks, like Citigroup of New York, NY, and Bank of America, headquartered in Charlotte, North Carolina, the two largest banks in the United States. Both were considered *"too big to fail"*.

2. **Securities Only Advisors** – Wall Street is a little different than the banking community, but their advisors have more in common than one might think. What do you think securities only advisors will recommend you do with your IRA? They will do the same thing the bank advisor would do: they will advise you to use the products they are paid to sell and recommend that you invest your IRA in securities. They will continue to recommend buying, holding, and trading securities in all market conditions, because that is what they do. If you are young and still building

your IRA account, this might be good advice. You have the luxury of time on your side, so you can ride out Wall Street's storms and hope that the market will grow over the long haul. This is the buy-and-hold approach investors commonly used in the past. After the 2008 Wall Street collapse, many experts are now saying that the buy and hold strategy is no longer a sound approach.

If you are retired or close to retirement, investing all of your IRA in securities could lead to IRA disaster. If you will need income from your IRA in the next five to ten years, investing all of your IRA in securities could be a costly mistake for most senior Americans. When you begin taking distributions from your retirement accounts, a drop in the market means taking a reduced income or running the risk that you will outlive your savings. In the case of an IRA, you will be forced to take Required Minimum Distributions no matter what the market conditions are. The one exception to this occurred in 2009. IRA owners were allowed to skip the Required Minimum Distributions for that year only. IRA owners who were forced to take a distribution in 2008 from accounts that had lost as much as 40% of their value know that a market meltdown can ruin the best laid retirement plans. In short, much like the bank advisor, most securities only advisors sell what they are paid to sell. Most are product oriented and don't have adequate training in IRA distribution planning.

3. **Certified Public Accountants** – CPAs are a great resource when it comes to tax preparation and tax planning. For many tax payers, their CPA is their most trusted advisor. The CPA or tax preparer hands them Form 1040, says *"Sign here and write a check for this amount to the IRS"*, and without hesitation, they do it. That takes a great deal of trust.

Some of the larger CPA firms have developed an in-house financial services division that offers securities and insurance products in addition to their tax preparation practice. For the most part they do a good job balancing investment risk for their younger clients with the need for safety for their senior clients.

This is all good but keep in mind, Form 1040 does not report what could or should have happened, it reports only what *did* happen. Often, what occurred is rapid IRA distribution causing rapid taxation and the loss of the *"Stretch Option"*. Do not assume that your CPA is trained to properly structure your IRA to take full advantage of the *"Stretch Option"* and generate the maximum income for you, your spouse, your children and grandchildren. When it comes to your IRAs and other qualified retirement accounts, most of the IRS deadlines fall on December 31. By the time your CPA or tax preparer gets to your return, the December 31 deadline will have come and gone.

DAVID F. ROYER

4. **Elder Law Attorneys** – Some attorneys specialize in dealing with senior's needs. Their primary tools to help seniors transfer wealth, reduce taxes, and accomplish many other goals are the use of different types of trusts and wills designed for senior clients. Trusts can be extremely effective in controlling your wealth after you're gone. The correct use of a trust can be beneficial in IRA planning, depending on your circumstances and wishes. For example, if you have a beneficiary who has special needs or will have difficulty managing an inherited IRA, a trust might be the best solution. Similarly, if there is the potential that one of your children or grandchildren will get divorced, you might need a trust to make sure that your IRA won't wind up in the hands of a soon to be ex-son-in-law. If you or your spouse have children from a prior marriage, a trust can be used to determine who will and who will not inherit your IRA. A trust can also be an effective tool for IRA charitable gifting. When it comes to IRA distribution planning, special rules apply regarding the use of trusts. Not knowing these rules can have a disastrous outcome for those wishing to take advantage of the "Stretch Option". First under IRS regulation 401-(a)(9)-4,A-5 the trust must adhere to four rules to be valid:

I. It must be valid under state law. This can be a problem if you have a trust made in one state then later relocate to another state. It's critical to make sure the trust is still valid in your new state of residence.

II. It must be irrevocable at death. This simply means that it cannot be changed after the IRA owner is deceased.

III. It must have identifiable beneficiaries.

IV. It must be provided to the custodian of your IRA no later than October 31 of the year after the IRA owner's death. If this deadline is missed, the *"Stretch Option"* will be lost.

Remembering all of these rules can be an obstacle to IRA distribution planning, but it gets worse. *"The Separate Account Rules cannot be used by beneficiaries of a trust."* This is stated two times in *IRS Publication 590*. This means that all beneficiaries will be treated as if they have the same life expectancy and will be limited to the stretch payout period of the oldest beneficiary. For example, if you have three IRA beneficiaries ages 55, 35 and 15, they will all be treated as if they were age 55. This will greatly decrease the income to the younger beneficiaries. Another important consideration is that, if at any point, a trust becomes the actual owner of your IRA, it will immediately become taxable.

Each of the rules about using a trust for your IRA is an opportunity to make mistakes that can cost you, and your beneficiaries, a fortune. Just like with CPAs, assuming your attorney is an IRA distribution expert can be a big mistake.

5. **Captive Advisors** – Some financial advisors are mandated to recommend whatever their employer dictates they must sell if they want to keep their jobs. Most bank and securities only advisors also fall into this category. Captive simply means they are employees of banks, brokerage firms, or insurance companies. They are restricted to the limited options offered by their employers. In simple terms, they work for their company, not for you.

6. **Insurance Advisors** – Insurance advisors fall into two categories, Captive agents and Independent agents. Captive insurance agents are employees of a particular insurance company. They typically can sell only the products offered by their company. This can be a handicap when it comes to offering the best advice for IRA distribution planning. The products offered by their company may not be the best product for you. Independent insurance agents are self-employed contractors who have the ability to choose which insurance companies they want to represent. Many independent insurance agents represent 20 or more insurance companies. This gives them a broader base of products and services to choose from, putting them at an advantage when it comes to

recommending the product that best fits your situation. Many insurance advisors are also licensed securities advisors. This gives them even greater flexibility when it comes to giving you the best advice for your particular situation.

7. **Independent Advisors** – This group of financial professionals has a unique advantage. They typically are licensed and trained in both insurance and securities and can offer you the entire universe of financial solutions. Many Independent Advisors are also trained and specialize in IRA/401(k) planning.

When considering the services of a financial professional to give you a second opinion; their training and expertise in IRA distribution and retirement planning solutions are what you and your family will benefit from the most.

With this understanding of the basic categories of advisors, this is what you should expect the financial professional to do when you get a second opinion:

• Check beneficiary designations on all retirement accounts and life insurance policies to make sure they are up-to-date.

• Review the downside potential of all of your investments to make sure it does not exceed your risk tolerance.

- Check for hidden fees and loads that will erode your retirement savings over time.

- Explain how your beneficiaries can take advantage of the *"Stretch Option"* and enjoy an income they cannot outlive.

- Make sure you are taking full advantage of tax deferred and tax-free IRA strategies.

- Help you avoid unnecessary taxes and IRS penalties.

Using the wrong or untrained advisor can be worse than having no advisor at all. The challenge is selecting an advisor that has the training and skills to help you get the maximum benefit from your retirement plans.

Have you ever noticed how easy it is to get inaccurate or just plain bad advice? *It's a lot like getting a bad haircut, but unlike the bad haircut, your retirement savings might not grow back.* Before following any advisor's advice about your IRA, make sure they are qualified to give you that advice.

Here are two quick tips that will help you choose the ideal advisor:

1. **Ask a lot of questions**. The ideal IRA advisor should be able to answer any questions you have about structuring your IRA or other qualified retirement plans. Asking questions is like

peeling an onion: the more layers you peel off, the more transparent the onion becomes. It works the same with financial advisors. Complete transparency is what you should be looking for. The deeper you dig, the more you will find out what they do or do not know about IRA planning.

2. **Don't base your decision solely on the advisor's experience**. Experience is a good thing to look for in an advisor, but experience alone won't tell you whether this is the right advisor for your IRA or 401(k). Some advisors may tout that they have 30 or 40 years of experience in the financial services industry, but this doesn't necessarily make them IRA experts. In some cases, it indicates only that they are survivors. Their training, more than their experience, is what matters when it comes to retirement planning. You are better off with an advisor with less experience who is a student of IRA distribution than one who has been doing the same thing for 30 years and has one year of experience 30 times. However, the advisor who possesses a combination of both experience and IRA training will be in the best position to offer you valuable advice.

Here are six questions you can ask a potential advisor to determine whether he or she is the right choice for you:

1. **What training do you have in IRA Distribution Planning?** Most financial advisors are generalists—they do a little bit of everything, from auto insurance to giving investment advice. IRS regulations are complex, and many dates and deadlines must be followed to avoid additional taxes and penalties. The Trained IRA Advisor should be able to elaborate on the formal IRA training courses they have attended. How frequently they participate in continuing education is also important. The tax rules change often and the savvy advisor knows the importance of staying current. They should attend updated IRA training meetings periodically to stay informed and be on their game.

2. **Do you have a copy of IRS Publication 590?** *IRS Publication 590* is the IRA rulebook and one of the best information sources for the trained advisor. The rulebook clarifies what you can and cannot do with your IRA. Your advisor should be able to show you all of the rules about how to properly designate beneficiaries, the correct way to do a Roth IRA Conversion, the problems related to using a will or a trust to designate your beneficiaries, and everything else that pertains to properly structuring your retirement accounts for maximum income and minimum taxes.

3. **Are you familiar with all areas of retirement and estate planning?** IRA rules are more complex than the rules for non-qualified retirement accounts, but your IRA is only part of the overall retirement picture. The ideal advisor will take into account all aspects of retirement and estate planning and should have the skills to ensure your IRA is working in harmony with your overall plans. Coordinating IRAs, 401(k) plans, non-qualified savings, and life insurance requires an advisor who is knowledgeable in all areas of retirement and estate planning.

4. **What happens to my IRA at death, the death of a beneficiary, or if one of the beneficiaries gets a divorce?** This question will help you determine whether the advisor is up-to-speed. The answers are dictated by your IRA custodial agreement and beneficiary document. Typically, at the IRA owner's death, the proceeds will be passed to the surviving spouse. If there is no surviving spouse, the IRA will likely pass to your children and/or grandchildren or other beneficiaries you have selected. If one of the Designated Beneficiaries predeceases the IRA owner, the beneficiary form will need to be amended. If one of your beneficiaries has a high likelihood of getting a divorce, this should be addressed now rather than later. For example, if your daughter inherits some of your IRA and resides in a community property

state and deposits her inheritance in a joint account, the outcome could be your ex-son-in-law will wind up with half of her inherited IRA. Remember, the beneficiary document trumps all other documents, including wills, trusts and decrees of divorce. It's critically important that your beneficiary documents are reviewed annually or when a triggering event occurs.

5. **Do you use the Team Approach?** Have you heard the expression, *"Too many cooks can spoil the stew"*? This is true, unless they are working in harmony and are all on the same page. Properly structuring your IRAs and other accounts often requires the services of more than one professional. Your family may benefit from a power of attorney, a will or a trust, which will require an attorney who deals in this area of law. You may also need the services of a CPA to make sure your financial planning is in harmony with tax planning. The ideal advisor will have relationships with other professionals and seek advice in their areas of expertise. Your advisor should always have the big picture and the knowledge to call the plays. Calling the wrong play often results in financial mistakes that cannot be reversed. Having a well-trained advisor spearheading the team will help you avoid conflicting advice that can make each decision more difficult than it needs to be.

6. **What are the three tables used to calculate Required Minimum Distributions?** This is an easy question for the trained advisor. The tables are in the back of *IRS Publication 590.*

Table I *(Single Life Expectancy)*
This is the table to be used by non-spousal beneficiaries, including children, grandchildren, and all beneficiaries other than your spouse.

Table II *(Joint Life and Last Survivor Expectancy)*
This table is for IRA owners whose spouses are more than 10 years younger than the IRA owner.
Table III *(Uniform Lifetime)*
This table is used to calculate the Required Minimum Distributions for Unmarried Owners, Married Owners whose spouses are not more than 10 years younger than the IRA owner, or Married Owners whose spouses are not the sole beneficiaries of their IRAs.

Using the wrong table to calculate Required Minimum Distributions could result in taking an insufficient distribution and paying the 50% Excise Tax on the missed portion. Remember from Mistake #1, if you miss a required distribution or take an insufficient distribution, close to 80% of the distribution in question could wind up in the hands of the IRS.

Here is a bonus question, you should ask yourself. Has your current advisor adequately explained the important IRA tax traps and opportunities discussed in this book? If the answer is no, it may be time to consider getting a second opinion. Keep in mind:

"It is impossible to get a second opinion from the same advisor who gave you the first one."

A second opinion from a Trained Independent IRA Advisor can make the difference between generations of reliable income and retirement disaster and help you avoid the Top 10 Mistakes made by IRA owners and their beneficiaries.

— BONUS CHAPTER —

IRAs, 401(k)s AND THE BOOMER GENERATION

Those who were born between 1946 and 1964 have the distinction of being *"Baby Boomers"*. As their parents would remember World War II, the Korean Conflict and the crooning of Frank Sinatra, Boomers are more likely to be tuned-in to Vietnam, the Beetles, Woodstock and electronic gadgets their parents never dreamed of owning. The Baby Boomer generation is close to 78 million strong, and anyone who sells anything has been targeting this demographic for as long as the expression *"Baby Boomer"* has been around. Approximately 10,000 Boomers are reaching retirement age every day and they will soon control the majority of the wealth of America. How well this generation manages this money is of enormous importance to everyone!

Many Boomers will have at least one, if not several, qualified retirement accounts, such as an IRA or 401(k). If you are a Boomer, you are part of the group with the highest probability of having your own IRA, 401(k), SEP, or all three, and also inheriting IRAs or 401(k)s from your parents. The IRA you own will need to be treated differently from the IRA you may inherit. The distribution rules are different for your personal IRA vs. an inherited IRA. In this area, making distribution mistakes can easily lead to costly IRS tax traps.

The IRA/401(k) You Own

Most Boomers made substantial contributions to their IRAs, 401(k)s, SEPs, and/or TSA 403(b) plans during their years in the workforce. Some may also have benefited from employer matching funds and grown their retirement account into a substantial retirement nest egg. The rules for the plans you contributed to are the same as the rules for your parents—the demographic Tom Brokaw dubbed *"The Greatest Generation"*. You pay no income tax on your contributions and you do not have to begin taking taxable distributions until the year after you turn age 70½. You can take advantage of the *"Stretch Option"* and enjoy a lifetime of income for you, your spouse, your children and grandchildren. Life is good.

Here is where it gets complicated. In addition to the IRA you own, you are likely to inherit a retirement account form one or both of your parents. Having these two different types of accounts can create income planning and distribution challenges. The distribution rules are substantially different for an IRA you own vs. an inherited IRA. When inheriting an IRA or other qualified retirement account the beneficiary will be faced with decisions that will need to be made quickly.

Managing the trillions of dollars of qualified retirement money in America is big business, and every potential custodian wants a bite of your retirement savings. Everyone will be ready to give you advice, but not all advisors are skilled in the distribution rules. It's like swimming in a shark tank and all of the sharks are saying the same thing in deep soothing voices, *"Be my friend and I'll protect you. The other sharks just want to take a big bite out of you"*. Acting on the wrong advice could lead to one of the many IRS tax traps. Armed with the right information, you will know who is giving sound financial advice and who to send packing.

The IRA/401(k) You Inherit

An inherited IRA or 401(k) must be treated differently than the IRA /401(k) you own and have contributed to. You cannot delay taking distributions from an inherited IRA or 401(k) until you are age 70½. You must take your first Required Minimum Distribution by December 31 of the year following the year you inherited the account. This is where common distribution mistakes can lead to higher taxes and unnecessary IRS penalties.

Inheriting an IRA

Fortunately, you are still in control of your money, even when you inherit an IRA or 401(k) account, and you can decide the best distribution method for your needs. You have two options:

Option 1

If you decide to use all of the money now from an inherited IRA, you will need to pay all of the income tax now and then do what you wish with what is left after the tax bite. If you are still working and having earned income, this approach could push you into a higher marginal tax bracket and tax away some of your earned income.

Option 2

Designated beneficiaries have the right to stretch the distributions of the inherited IRA over their individual life expectancies and take advantage of the *"Stretch Option"*. However, if you want to spread the distributions and taxes over your life expectancy, you cannot become the owner of the inherited IRA or roll the inherited IRA into your personal IRA. Remaining a beneficiary is the only approach that allows non-spousal beneficiaries to spread the distributions and distribution taxes over their life expectancies. Stretching the distributions from an inherited IRA is a powerful tool for those who desire a life time of income and also want to spread out the taxes. Each year income tax will need to be paid only on the amount that is distributed rather than paying the full tax bill in one year.

Choosing to stretch the distributions for now does not prevent you from changing your mind later. The entire account, or any portion of the account, can be liquidated at any time, if you are willing to pay the income tax. If you decide to take only the Required Minimum Distributions, you must take the first minimum distribution by December 31 of the year after the account owner's death. Future required distributions must be taken before December 31 of each subsequent year. If the December 31 deadline is missed, taxes will still be owed for the missed distribution, in addition to the 50% Excise Tax described in Mistake #1. Keep in mind, the longer you are able to defer the tax on an inherited IRA, the longer it will continue to earn interest on money that otherwise would have been paid to the IRS.

You should note that after inheriting an IRA, under current IRS rules, you cannot convert the inherited IRA to a Roth IRA.

Inheriting a 401(k) or other Company-Sponsored Plan

Inheriting a company-sponsored retirement account can be a little more complicated than inheriting an IRA. Most 401(k) plans have no provision that will allow non-spousal beneficiaries to take advantage of the *"Stretch Option"*. 401(k) plans typically require non-spousal beneficiaries to take an immediate taxable distribution or a five-year payout.

Prior to 2006 non-spousal beneficiaries of 401(k) plans were required to take full distribution and pay all of the income tax by the fifth anniversary of the 401(k) owner's death. Put simply, they would have to settle with the tax man in just five years. This rule created rapid distribution causing rapid taxation. Non-spousal beneficiaries of 401(k) plans were treated like disenfranchised, redheaded stepchildren. Spousal beneficiaries have the right to roll the 401(k) to an IRA, but the children and grandchildren were stuck with the five-year payout. If you inherited a 401(k) from anyone other than your spouse, the IRS rules were like shifting sands. Fortunately, a series of events that began in 2006 would ultimately lead to more flexible income options for inheriting non-spousal beneficiaries— but the road to get there took several detours.

April 17, 2006, the *Pension Protection Act* (PPA) was signed into law. The PPA included a special provision for non-spousal beneficiaries of a 401(k) and other company sponsored retirement plans. It stated that non-spousal beneficiaries, beginning in 2007, would have the right to transfer the inherited 401(k) to a properly structured IRA. This provision made it possible for non-spousal beneficiaries to stretch the distributions and the taxes over their individual life expectancies. It further stated that this must be done in a certain manner. It could not be a rollover. It must be a trustee to trustee transfer. That means that the funds must go directly from the 401(k) custodian to the new custodian of your choosing. Titling the new IRA is also critical. The IRA must be issued in the name of the deceased as owner, for the benefit of you, the beneficiary. This important piece of legislation gave the inheriting non-spousal beneficiary the right to move the 401(k) to an IRA and take advantage of the *"Stretch Option"*.

January 10, 2007, the IRS issued notice 2007-7. This clarification stated that 401(k) custodians are not forced to comply with the *Pension Protection Act*, taking you right back where you started, paying the taxes within five years. It gets even more frustrating.

October 24, 2007, the IRS changed their position again. They stated that beginning in 2008, the non-spousal provisions of the *Pension Protection Act* effecting inherited 401(k) plans would become mandatory. So again, you would have the right to transfer the inherited 401(k) to a properly structured IRA and could stretch the distribution and taxes over your life expectancy. The IRS waffled once more, and this ruling was not enforced. At that point, non-spousal beneficiaries who inherited 401(k)s and other company sponsored retirement accounts were again forced to pay the taxes in five years. If that isn't enough to make anyone crazy, here is the latest.

December 23, 2008, an election year, both the House and the Senate unanimously voted for the passage of *The Worker, Retiree, and Employer Recovery Act of 2008*. Under this act, all employer sponsored plans, including 401(k)s, will be required to allow non-spousal beneficiaries to do direct rollovers to properly titled inherited IRAs, effective after December 31, 2009. This means you, as a non-spousal beneficiary, can do a direct rollover of an inherited 401(k) and most other company sponsored plans to an IRA, beginning in 2010. Finally, there was a way to get around the five-year rule and non-spousal beneficiaries who inherited 401(k) plans could transfer to an IRA and enjoy the tax-deferral advantages of the *"Stretch Option"*.

A Case in Point:

Frank, an old friend of mine, invited me to his 60th birthday party in 2010. I had not seen Frank since the last class reunion we both attended more than 15 years ago, but we spoke occasionally by phone. He looked great and didn't appear to have aged much in the past 15 years. After talking with Frank, I realized that he would be the perfect poster boy for the Baby Boomer generation. His positive attitude was absolutely contagious. Not once did he complain, but he said some interesting things that convinced me that the Boomer generation is arguably the most unique generation of our time.

He made it clear that he would never get sick, never grow old, and that 60 is the new 40. He had no intention of downsizing his house or even thinking about retiring. Frank intended to work until he dropped.

During our visit, Frank told me about his father's passing in December of the prior year, just two years after losing his mother. His father worked for a retail store until he was 72 and would have worked longer, but his health was failing. The store offered its employees a 401(k) plan, with 50% employer matching funds, so Frank's father made the maximum contribution each year. At his father's death, at age 82, there was $347,000 remaining in his 401(k) and Frank, being an only child, was the sole beneficiary.

When the 401(k) custodian contacted Frank, they explained that his father had taken his required distribution for the year of death and Frank would need to decide what to do with the remaining balance. They told him he had two options: Take full distribution and pay all of the taxes now or take the money before the end of the fifth year after his father's death, allowing Frank to spread the taxes over five years. Frank chose the latter to keep his current tax bill as low as possible. I asked Frank if they explained that he had a third option. Frank could have transferred the 401(k) to an inherited IRA and spread the distributions and taxes over his remaining life expectancy of 25.2 years. The 401(k) custodian did not explain the third option. Fortunately we caught this one in time. Frank had until the end of 2010 to transfer the 401(k) to an IRA and take his first Required Minimum Distribution.

The moral of this story is: You can't depend on the advice of minimum wage employees of the custodians of 401(k) plans. Even though under *The Worker, Retiree, and Employer Recovery Act of 2008*, Frank had the right to make the transfer and enjoy the benefits of a more flexible IRA, the employee of the plan custodian was not up to speed and Frank was about to make a costly mistake.

If you are going to inherit a 401(k) or other company sponsored plans from your parents or grandparents, I recommend having an open conversation with them to discuss the best way to make your inheritance uncomplicated and tax advantaged. Everyone involved, including your advisor, should be on the same page when it comes to minimizing taxes and maximizing the income from your inheritance.

Unlike an inherited IRA, you do have the option to convert an inherited 401(k) to a Roth IRA and enjoy tax free growth and income tax free distributions.

5 Rules for Non-spousal Beneficiaries to Avoid IRS Tax Traps:

1. Non-spousal beneficiaries cannot become the owner of an inherited IRA or deposit it into their own IRA. Making either of these mistakes will cause the inherited IRA to become immediately taxable.

2. Non-spousal beneficiaries cannot make any contributions to an inherited IRA.

3. Non-spousal beneficiaries cannot delay taking distributions from an inherited IRA until they turn age 70½. Their first required distribution must be taken before December 31 of the year after the owner's death. If this deadline is missed, the beneficiary will owe a 50% Excise Tax in addition to the income tax on the missed distribution.

4. If there is more than one non-spousal beneficiary, the inherited IRA must be divided into separate accounts, with separate beneficiaries, for each beneficiary to be able to use their individual life expectancy and take full advantage of the *"Stretch Option"*. Separate accounts with separate beneficiaries must be established no later than December 31 of the year after the IRA owner's death.

5. If the deceased account owner was past their Required Beginning Date *(April 1 of the year after turning age 70½)* and had not taken the required distribution during the year of death, the inheriting non-spousal beneficiaries must take a distribution equal the distribution the IRA owner would have taken if still living.

If you are a Baby Boomer and have contributed to an IRA, 401(k), SEP, 403(b), 457(b) or any other qualified retirement plan and have inherited or expect to inherit a qualified plan, seek help from an advisor who specializes in IRA inheritance and distribution.

SUMMARY

IRAs, SEPs, 401(k)s, 403(b)s, 457 plans, and all other qualified retirement accounts have different and more complicated rules than regular savings accounts. The tax codes governing these accounts are filled with two things: tax traps and gold nuggets. The purpose of this book is to help you navigate the minefields of rules, regulations, and deadlines and pick up all of the gold nuggets that are available to you.

Let's start by reviewing the important dates and deadlines that will affect your retirement accounts and the tax traps you can avoid.

While the IRA owner is living:

60 days to complete an IRA rollover.

Only One IRA Rollover per IRA per year

Age 59½ is when the IRA owner can take distributions without paying the pre-59½, 10% early withdrawal penalty.

April 1 of the year following the year the owner turns age 70½ is the Required Beginning Date (RBD) to take your first Required Minimum Distribution (RMD).

December 31 is the deadline for all future RMDs.

October 15 of the year following the year of the Roth IRA Conversion is the deadline for recharacterization.

The year following the IRA owner's death:

September 30 is the deadline for determining designated beneficiaries for the purpose of taking advantage of the *"Stretch Option"*.

October 31 is the deadline for providing a copy of the trust to the IRA custodian.

December 31 is the deadline for non-spousal beneficiaries to take their first RMD and to establish Separate Accounts to avoid using the life expectancy of the oldest beneficiary.

Missing any of these important dates and deadlines can result in rapid taxation, additional IRS penalties, and the loss of tax saving strategies.

Now that we have that behind us, let's start picking up those gold nuggets that you can use to create IRA opportunities for you and your family.

The *"Stretch Option"*
This is clearly a gold nugget in the tax code that can transform your IRA into a lifetime of income for three generations. A $200,000 IRA can

generate more than $1 million of income for you and your family. The RMD was reduced in 2002, so more money likely will be left to be passed on to your heirs, and now they can turn their inheritance into a lifetime of income. It's like giving them a birthday present every year for the rest of their lives. It does not cost anything to take advantage of this opportunity. You only need to make sure your beneficiary documents are set up properly. Additional information can be found in Mistake #2.

Controlling Investment Risk

If you are retired or nearing retirement, too much risk can ruin your plans. The market has the potential of great rewards, but it is counterbalance by the potential of loss. Take the time to examine the potential downside of your investments to be certain it does not exceed your risk tolerance. For additional information, review Mistake #5.

Control the Fees and Loads

In Mistake #6 you learned that fees and loads can erode your nest egg over time. Gambling with too much of your retirement savings is bad enough, but if Las Vegas charged a fee to enter a casino, would you pay it? The closer you are to retirement, the more you may need to reduce unnecessary expenses.

The Roth IRA Conversion

This is an extra large nugget in the tax code. If you won't need your IRA for income, you should consider converting at least some of your IRA to a Roth. A small tax bite now could save a fortune of tax dollars in the future. If you are going to consider converting, do it before the tax brackets are increased. Remember from Mistake #7, after a Roth IRA conversion the IRS is completely out of the picture and you can take control of your IRA. All future gains and qualified distributions will be income tax free for you and your heirs.

IRA Arbitrage

One of the greatest gifts in the tax code is that life insurance death benefits are income tax free. If your goal is to pass more to your family, you can use the after tax IRA balance to leverage larger and tax-free life insurance benefits. Life insurance is the cornerstone of sound financial planning. Remember from Mistake #7, the money used to pay for life insurance does not disappear. The life insurance cash values are there if you need money for income or unexpected expenses. Review Mistake #7 for all of the additional benefits life insurance can offer, including the funding of Long-Term Care expenses.

Rolling 401(k) and 403(b) Plans to an IRA

The reasons for owning company-sponsored plans are gone after you retire. The IRS allows you to move the funds in restrictive 401(k) and 403(b) plans to the more flexible IRA. Rolling your plan to an IRA opens up the floodgate of investment options and gives you and your family greater income planning flexibility. Review Mistake #8 for all of the advantages of retiring your company sponsored plans when you retire.

Consolidating Retirement Accounts

This was addressed in Mistake #9. Having too many retirement accounts can become a retirement nightmare. The IRS allows you to consolidate your 401(k)s, 403(b) plans, and all other qualified investments into one easily managed IRA. The more retirement accounts you own, the more likely you will miss an important date or deadline. Consolidation is one of the most effective ways to avoid unnecessary taxes and IRS penalties. Remember, IRAs, Roth IRAs, and non-qualified savings accounts must be kept separate.

Getting a Second Opinion

This is not a nugget in the tax code but it is something you owe to yourself. The IRS minefield of regulations, deadlines, and penalties is not going to go away. This was discussed in Mistake #10. If you own a qualified retirement account, you are faced with navigating the minefield while you collect all of the gold nuggets that are available to you. A second opinion from a qualified advisor will tell you if you are on the right track.

Remember, your retirement savings is *your* money. You don't need to let Uncle Sam become a senior partner in your IRAs and other retirement plans. By taking the time and following the steps recommended in this book to plan and structure your IRA accounts properly, you can safeguard your wealth for *your* retirement years and provide a comfortable financial future for your loved ones.